Golf with your Hands

Golf with your Hands

LOUIS T. STANLEY

with a Foreword by Gary Player

and photographs by the author

Thomas Y. Crowell Company

New York · Established 1834

First published in the United States of America in 1967

Printed in Great Britain

L.C. Card 67-17244

Contents

Contents

Foreword by Gary Player

It gives me great pleasure to write this Foreword, for I have known Louis Stanley for many years and am an admirer of his writing. A scratch golfer, he has given considerable thought to the techniques of the game. Over the years he has studied, analysed and played with many of the greatest players; in fact, no golfer of international repute has escaped the lens of his camera. Louis Stanley's previous book, *Swing to Better Golf*, was a best-seller. In this volume he concentrates on the role of the hands, emphasizing the basic fact that a sound grip is essential. Without it, one's game can never improve. He demonstrates with a lavish collection of photographs taken in championships and tournaments all over the world, how hand placement must be correct for every shot. His camera has frozen the hands at various stages of the swing, particularly at the top of the backswing. He stresses, quite rightly, that the grip is essentially personal, but once chosen, the hand placement must be right, and in this book Louis Stanley tells how this can be done.

Golf with your Hands will improve your game. It is simple to understand—the clarity of the explanations is one of its strongest points—and I recommend it warmly to every class of golfer.

Introduction

Golf has become over-complicated. There are far too many would-be short cuts to perfection, bait to a gullible golfer struggling to break 100. Before playing a stroke, he must remember to stay down over the shot, to check the right hip, to flex his left leg, not to slug, to be rhythmic, to control the right hand, to position the right shoulder and elbow, to hood the wedge, to lob the pitch, keep head down, follow-through, and so on. No wonder the poor fellow is bemused. Nobody could assimilate such a solid diet of advice. The task is impossible. The average reaction-time for a nerve impulse to send an order from brain to muscle varies according to the individual but a fast reaction-time is one-fifth of a second. The time taken from the top of the backswing to the moment of impact is two-fifths of a second. On that reckoning, only two tips can be mulled over in the reaction-time available, and I would say that ideally two is one too many.

It is better to cut out confusing advice and concentrate on the basic fundamental of the game, the cardinal point of all successful shot-making; focus attention on the hands and get them functioning properly. By all means read about the role played by the hips, shoulders, back muscles, leg muscles, and the rest. Each has its contribution to make in the shot, but if the hands are working as they should, all these trimmings fall into place without conscious effort. The finest golf is played when the entire swing is subconscious.

The hands hold the secret of golf. They are the only part of the body to come into contact with the club. The basic factor is the grip. The way your hands are placed on the club determines the degree of control you have over a shot, and decides direction and distance. A faulty grip is the commonest cause of poor golf, just as it is true to say that there is no first-class player who does not have enviable hand-action. In a way it is a vicious circle. Clubhead speed is essential if you are going to play a good shot, but it is impossible to get clubhead speed unless you use your hands. Clubhead speed is injected through the hands. A sound grip is therefore essential if your game is to improve.

I remember J. H. Taylor's words on this topic, "As far as possible put your brains into your hands. Let the ankles, knees and hips do their swinging movement as subconsciously as possible, and let your thoughts live only in your hands." Excellent advice. If your grip is faulty it is impossible for arms, elbows, shoulders, body, legs and feet to function properly. I do not suggest there is only one correct way to grip a club. There are several, the final choice often being affected by the size and shape

Introduction

of the hands, and length of fingers, but the one used by the majority of top-flight golfers is the overlapping grip.

Until you get used to it the hands feel clumsy, but after a time the grip becomes moulded to the shaft. The main thing is to concentrate on accurate hand placement. You can check it yourself quite easily. First of all, hold the shaft with the left hand. When the "V" formed by the index finger and thumb points over the right shoulder the hand is right. It ensures a strong finger-grip as opposed to the weaker palm-grip. Moreover, the left-hand positioning should have three knuckles visible. When the right hand is added, a similar "V" also points in the same direction. This prevents the right hand being too far under the shaft. Not only must the grip be sound, the pressure of the fingers must also be right. In that sense golf is a pressure game. The grip is firm, but not rigid, for that can only result in tension, and over-tense fingers mean over-tightened arm muscles. A golfer comes to know the power and feel of a golf club through his hands. His grip must be firm, yet sensitive. *The key fingers of the grip are the last three of the left hand.* These are the ones that decide whether the shot is going to be good or fluffed.

I refer to the action studies. The men and women I have chosen represent not only a great many years of golfing history, but between them reflect the cream of the world's top-flight golfing wisdom. The sum-total is a wealth of beautifully developed techniques perfected after years of constant practice. Studied and analysed with an intelligent appreciation of relevant detail, they constitute an almost complete golfing education. It is interesting to reflect that the players themselves went through the movements more or less subconsciously in a manner that "J.H." would have approved. We can study the visual evidence of what was happening. High-speed photography can freeze the swing at any point, but the players cannot isolate such sections, nor are their minds cluttered with tags and clichés.

Study the backswings and you can see how each player cocks his left wrist at the top of the swing. From this position there is freedom of action—pliability—something to hit with. If the left wrist was not allowed to bend or get into the correct position, the chance of hitting a good shot would be remote. You cannot fire an uncocked gun and you cannot hit with an uncocked wrist. The reason is simple. Your hands are the only part of the body to touch the club. Your wrists are the main hinges connecting the action of the hands with the action of the body. And they must all work together. If the wrists are stiffened-up, locked and out of action, how can the hands and body

Introduction

work together? How can you open a door when the hinges won't work? You can break it down, which is what the average golfer tries to do in getting the clubhead to and through the ball. He tries to break something down, to force his way through.

The main action must take place with the left wrist, since the left hand and left arm take the club back. There is no turning over of the hands to be done. The idea is to get the left hand well over the club, and then no pronating is needed. The backswing comes back well inside the line of flight, the hands close to the body and the left side turning. As the top of the swing is reached—short or long—the left wrist is then cocked and ready. From this position there is a feeling of both power and control. But if the left wrist is stiff or rigid at the top, with no sign of giving, then the hands must quit work and the body will attempt to take over the swing—with the usual results.

This is all simple enough for anyone who cares to take a little time to think about it, to study it, and to work it out. The illustrations show what happens. Those vital three fingers of the left hand are firm at the top of the backswing. There is no sign of loosening, no wrist flabbiness, no fluttering, but an overall impression of firmness.

Most golfers hit too soon. They uncoil the wrists long before the hands have moved into the hitting area. Power is expended before the clubhead reaches the ball. An overpowering right hand twists the clubface out of position and frequently cuts across the line. Again the solution lies with the grip. Get that hand placement accurate and there is no temptation to let the right hand take over too soon. Those three fingers of the left hand are the best safeguard. Experience shows that when the grip is firm, and the right hand infuses power in the hitting area, shoulder, hip and footwork automatically tend to co-ordinate with the hand action. Both hands work together and bring the clubface into the ball squarely at right angles to the desired line of flight. The final answer is practice, practice, practice, until the action becomes automatically natural. Above all, take your time. A hurried stroke is invariably an indifferent shot. And remember that a sound grip is the most valuable single asset in the golf bag, the key to shot-improvement.

Gary Player (South Africa)　　　　*Arnold Palmer (USA)*

1. The Vital Coupling

The role played by hands in the golf swing is vital. It is impossible to over-emphasize the importance of the grip. It is the key to successful golf. That does not mean there is a standardized grip. It is tempting to dogmatize, but individual preferences, plus physical limitations, such as finger-length, size of hands, forearm development and so on, make the choice of grip a purely personal one. Generally speaking, there are three recognized grips, plus a variety of variations introduced by the person holding the club. It could be the overlapping or Vardon grip, with the right hand little finger riding on and between the first and second finger knuckles of the left hand . . . the interlocking grip with the right hand little finger and left-hand forefinger interlocked . . . the palm-grip with the club lying in the palm of the hands. There are others, but usually the choice lies between the first two. I would give the casting vote to the overlapping grip.

Analyse the examples given. Each one has proved its worth to the player concerned. Generally speaking, there is only one way of placing the hands on the shaft, irrespective of the grip chosen. Note the left hand. However much the right hand may vary, the left is usually uniform. There is no suggestion of over-tenseness. On the other hand, it is not slack. It is a grip. However powerful may be the shot, there is no danger of the shaft turning in the hands when the clubface makes contact with the ball. It is imperative that it should be a grip, and not an apology for one. *The club must be gripped firmly*. At all costs avoid the piccolo touch with fingers loosened at the top of the backswing or during the follow-through. Hand placement is important. If the right hand gets too far over the shaft, the length of the shot will be affected. Should the back of the right hand be too far under the shaft, any hint of scissor-movement or rolling of the right wrist will shut the clubface and cause the shot to be pulled. When the left hand is too far over, the chances are that the shot will be sliced. Player, Palmer and Nicklaus are sound examples of how to hold the club at address.

The advice is worth repeating. *The grip must be firm*, but the wrists remain pliable. Until the hands are correct, there is no point in talking about the rest of the swing.

Jack Nicklaus (USA)

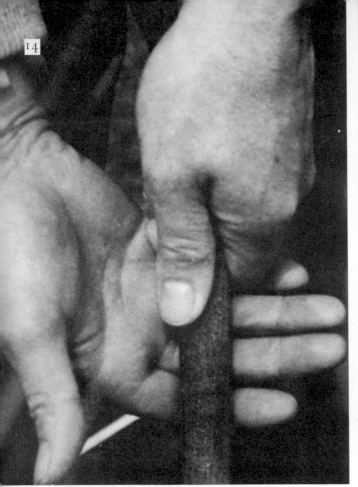
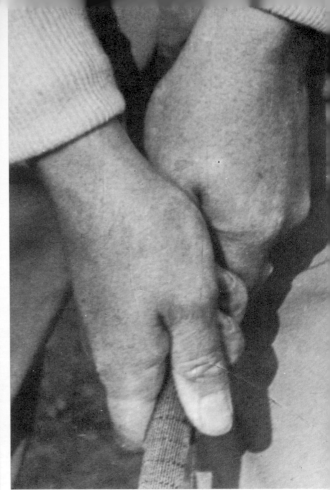
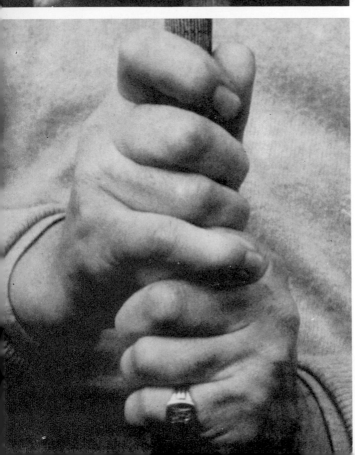

Ronnie White (England)

Flory van Donck (Belgium)

Lloyd Mangrum (USA)

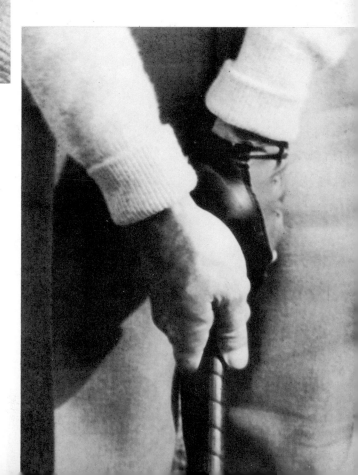

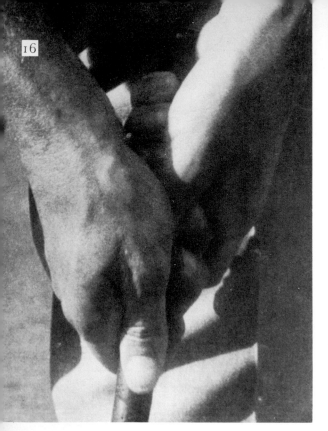
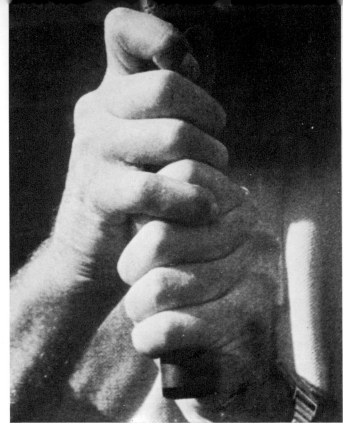

Bill Campbell (USA)

Richard Yost (USA)

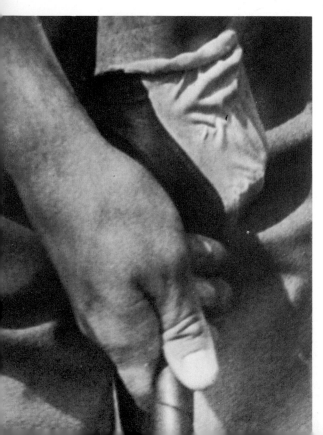
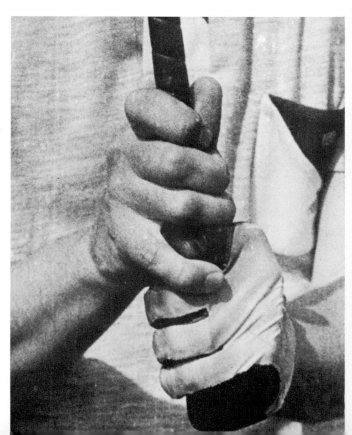

Lawson Little (USA)

Lawson Little (USA)

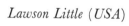

Lawson Little (USA)

Sam Urzetta (USA)

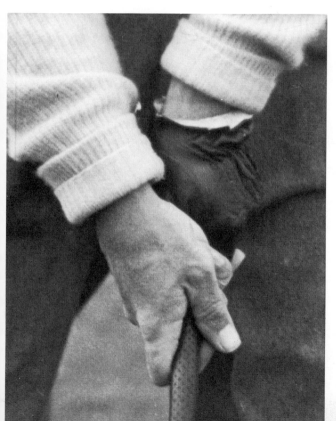

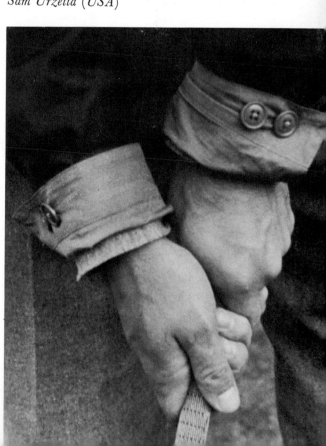

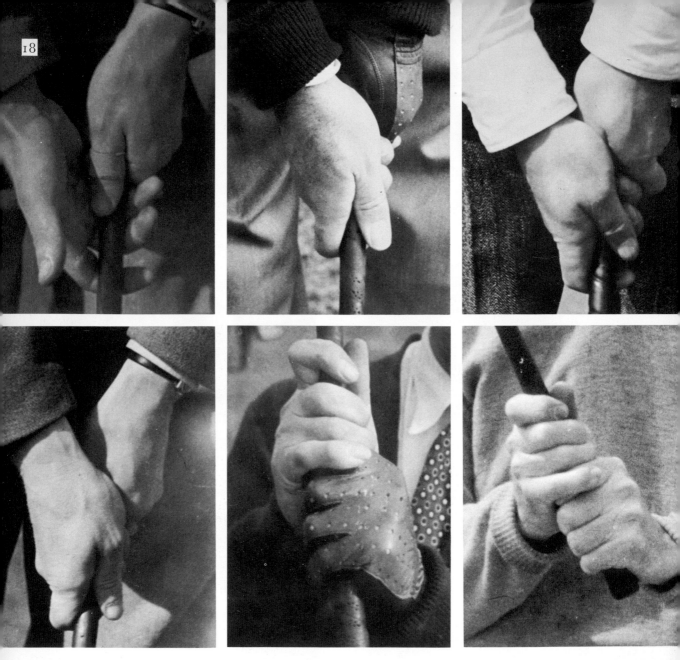

Tom Haliburton (Scotland)   *Syd Scott (England)*   *(Above) Fred Daly (Ireland)*

(Below) Peter Thomson (Australia)

19

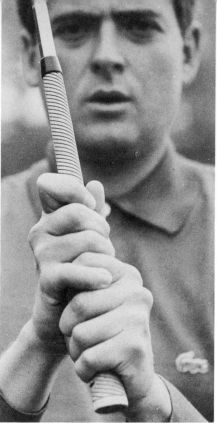

Hsieh Yung-Yo (China)   Gaetan Morgue d'Algue (France)   Chen Ching-Po (China)

George Will (Scotland)

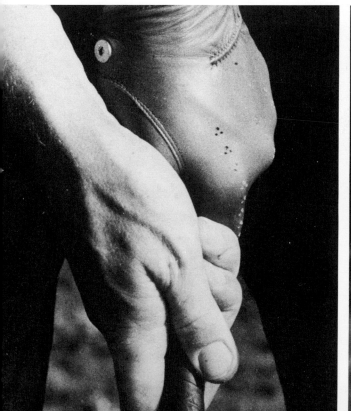

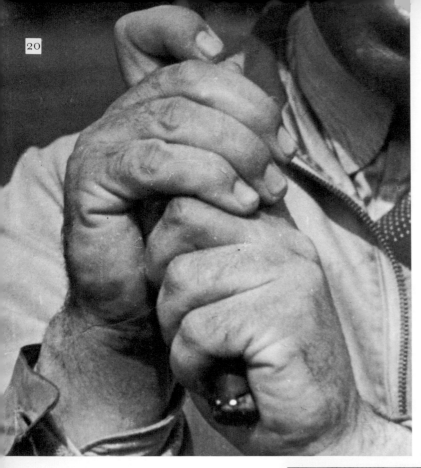

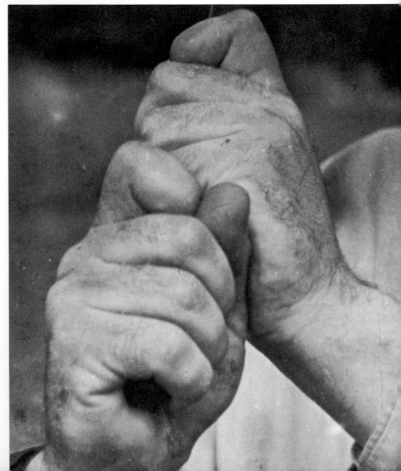

2. Unorthodox Grips

These unorthodox grips belong to Harry Bradshaw. One is a throw-back to the days when he played hurley. He found when he turned to golf that the instinctive grip was to hold the club the reverse way with the right hand at the top of the shaft. It looked eccentric and decidedly clumsy, but proved effective. The Irishman maintains that if you want your left arm to be really straight in the backswing this reverse grip does the trick. He decided to discard the grip when he came to England for tournament play. Had he persisted with it, there is no doubt it was a gimmick headline. So to avoid unwanted publicity, Bradshaw adopted an orthodox grip. The switch-over was not particularly happy. It felt strange and affected shot-making. Once more he experimented, eventually adopting a grip in which the last three fingers of the right hand overlap the left. It sounds strange, looks cumbersome, but has proved most effective. Try it out with a few practice shots.

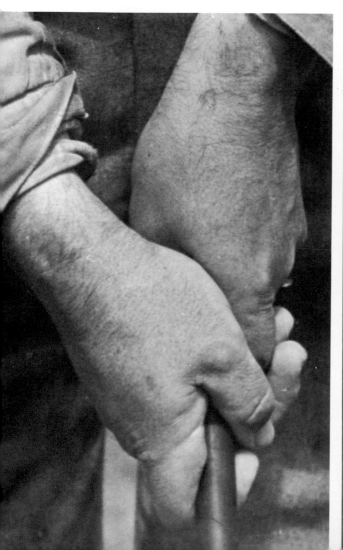 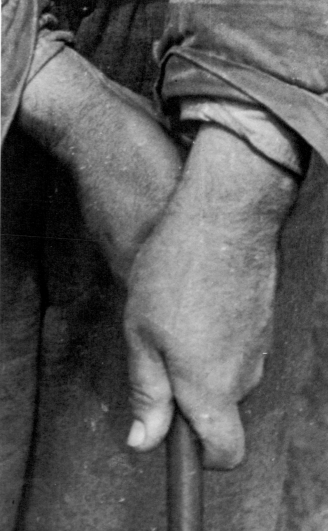

(*a and b*) *Jack Nicklaus* (*USA*)   (*c and d*) *Malcolm Gregson* (*England*)   (*e and f*) *Dick Meyer* (*USA*)

3. Muscle Loosening and Wrist Strengthening

No round should begin without a warm-up spell, yet the majority of golfers are stone-cold when they step on the first tee. Stiff muscles strangle any swing. Apart from going through a systematic drill of about forty practice shots, ranging from wood to short irons and pitches, finishing with some practice putts, here are a few variations. Jack Nicklaus (*a* and *b*) stretched his muscles with the aid of an iron, at the same time letting his body turn to and fro as if playing a shot. Malcolm Gregson (*c* and *d*), one of the most promising of the younger British professionals, goes through a routine of swinging a driver with his left hand. The right hand is tucked away in a trouser pocket. Dick Meyer (*e* and *f*), 1957 American Open champion, goes through the movements of a stroke with his right hand only. It is interesting to compare the two positions when he played the actual shot. Gene Sarazen (*g*), that ageless chubby character, warms up by swinging two clubs. Retief Waltman (*h*), the young South African whose game is so rich in promise, adopts the same method. Not only does it loosen stiff muscles, but as a form of exercise is admirable for strengthening arms and wrists.

(*g*) *Gene Sarazen (USA)*　　　　　　　　　　(*h*) *Retief Waltman (South Africa)*

4. Grip and Stance Drill

This is a selection of golfing idiosyncrasies, the individualistic drill that players go through before they are ready to play the stroke. Soling the club behind the ball is often the first step towards lining-up the stroke. That is a point that many club golfers overlook. If the club rests on its heel or toe the chances are that the club will twist in the hands as heel or toe makes contact with the ground. It is like driving a car on two wheels. Another method, as you can see in the illustrations, is to put the right foot forward, look at the line of flight, place the left foot in its stance position, and check the grip until it feels that both hands are moulded to the shaft. This may seem trifling, but remember that professionals of the calibre of Palmer (*e*), Hunt (*d*), Butler (*c*), Souchak (*a*), Poulsen (*b*), Sanders (*f*), and many others do not waste their time and thought on inessentials.

(*a*) *Mike Souchak (USA)*   (*c*) *Peter Butler (England)*   (*e*) *Arnold Palmer (USA)*

(*b*) *Carl Poulsen (Denmark)*   (*d*) *Bernard Hunt (England)*   (*f*) *Doug Sanders (USA)*

5. *The Stranahan Routine*

I have already stressed the value of adopting a set drill of pre-stance actions. To the onlooker they may seem so much waste of time. On the contrary, an automatic routine creates a sense of rhythmic purpose. It helps to co-ordinate mind and muscle, mentally shaping and playing the shot before actually squaring-up to the ball. Frank Stranahan had the temperament to adopt such a set pattern. At his peak he personified ruthless determination, a quality that sometimes led to misunderstandings. Admired by many, criticized by others, censured by a few, the American mirrored the maxim that you should never trust the collective wisdom of individual ignorance. Here was a young man with the self-assurance of a veteran sauntering with supreme indifference through life with a golf club in his hand. Like Mr. Pitt, he took the line, "the atrocious crime of being a young man I shall neither attempt to palliate nor deny". He treated his youth and strength as talismans of success. There was nothing wrong in that attitude.

I did not profess to understand his extraordinary devotion to the game. I have never seen any man spend so many hours, day after day, hitting golf balls into space. There was obviously some inner urge that would neither be satisfied nor stilled until the goal was reached. What that target was only Stranahan could say. I have a feeling that he wanted to emulate Bobby Jones, i.e. win the four major golfing titles in the same year. He was an extraordinary golfer to study and analyse. The swing had been so regimented that the mechanism bordered upon that of an automaton. With the possible exception of Cotton, no golfer in these islands, amateur or professional, and few in America could equal his tournament experience. I like Stranahan. I admired his single-mindedness, although I could not understand it. His success did not consist

of the sum total of the number of shots he made in a year, for, whatever the sage may have said, genius is never an affair of accountancy. It was a unique ability to concentrate on a subject to the exclusion of everything else.

6. Grip and Stance Check

Stance and address are important, but, like the grip, cannot be standardized. For instance, there is no uniformity in the width of stance. Long-handicap golfers are inclined to bestraddle the ball with feet too wide apart. The feeling of security may be reassuring, but it rules out any suggestion of a full pivot. The shot becomes an affair of shoulder and arms, with the back muscles locked and left side and hip swivel severely curtailed. Another fault to be eliminated is the tendency to creep ahead of the ball. A safe generalization is to say that for a full shot the feet should be about the width of the shoulders apart. Distance narrows as the shot gets shorter. As the loft of the club increases so the ball is addressed nearer to the right foot. In this way it is not necessary to compensate the hand action, the club graduation and altered ball position do it for you.

(a) *Jack Nicklaus (USA)*   (c) *Lloyd Mangrum (USA)*   (e) *Walter Burkemo (USA)*

(b) *Bruce Devlin (Australia)*   (d) *Ken Bousfield (England)*   (f) *Ted Kroll (USA)*

Al Balding (Canada)

Douglas Ford (USA)

7. Grip and Clubhead Check

Points to note: the position of the body in relation to the ball. Relaxed knees have eased any suggestion of body tension. Toes point out slightly. Arms hang naturally from the shoulders with the club acting as a natural extension, a position that generally makes a grooved swing easier. The wrists have full flexibility to act as a hinge linking arms and hands with the shaft and clubhead. Balding addresses the ball a fraction off the toe of the club. This tip can be useful if you want to make sure that the clubhead makes contact with the ball plumb in the centre of the face. During the swing the arms are fully extended, a degree of muscular stretching that does the trick. One of the things a golfer has to realize is that reaching out for the ball upsets balance. It is a well-known maxim that position at impact and address is virtually identical.

David Thomas (Wales) 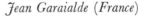 *Jean Garaialde (France)*

8. Hands Ahead in Address

A small point, but important. Study these photographs and note the angle of the shaft. It will be seen that the hands are a fraction ahead of the clubhead. Not only does this firm-up the left-hand grip, but it assists in bringing the clubface square to the line of flight at impact. Mention must be made of the placement of thumbs on the shaft. There is no such thing as the "right" place. Some players grip with the thumbs along the top of the shaft, others down the side, or round it. A former Open champion takes his right thumb off the shaft completely. Another professional is a first-class shot-maker in spite of having his left thumb amputated as a result of an accident. Extremists maintain that thumbs are useless passengers. Here is a specialized thumb tip as a postscript. Many golfers are inclined to overswing. At the top of the backswing the club falls limply over the shoulder. The arms have no control over the club. It has swung below the horizontal. The odds are that the hands will be too far ahead of the clubhead. Result—a feeble shot. If this is your trouble, place the right thumb straight down the top of the shaft. At the top of the backswing the thumb will be under the shaft and will act as a check to overswinging.

(Opposite) Peter Thomson (Australia)

Ronnie Shade (Scotland)   *Jim McHale (USA)*   *Martin Posse (Argentine)*

34

(a) David
Blair
(Scotland)

9. Avoid Tension

A player's mental attitude unquestionably affects play. Many a sliced, hooked or topped shot is due to over-tension on the tee, a general tightening-up that ruins a swing. The cause could be a faulty grip or stance. Some players hold the club so awkwardly that a rhythmic action is impossible. Others grip the shaft with frozen determination. Their arms are as stiff as pokers. Tension has left their muscles rigid. There are many players I could choose to illustrate the cure for this trouble, but the three selected are particularly relaxed golfers. Whatever happened to David Blair (a) on the links—success, failure, or even disaster—his calm was always complete. In this study his stance is evenly balanced. The arms hang naturally from the shoulders with the club acting as a natural extension. Study the position of the right hand on the shaft, particularly the forefinger and thumb.

It takes all sorts to make the golfing world, but few are as quiet and retiring in manner as Ken Bousfield (b). He makes the perfect foursomes partner, has exceptional ability and an ideal temperament. His is a copybook stance, completely free from tension. Ossie Pickworth (c), burly Australian professional, is just as relaxed. Study the hands and grip. Well did Vardon refer to the hands as the chief point of concentration for successful golf. If your grip is right and tension-free, you can build on a sound foundation.

(b) *Ken Bousfield* (*England*)   (c) *Ossie Pickworth* (*Australia*)

10. Reaching Destroys Balance

This tip follows naturally from the advice on the previous page. Muscular tension destroys a rhythmic swing. The ideal to adopt is the Blair image of a relaxed address position with the arms hanging naturally from the shoulders, the club virtually a natural extension. The main thing is not to exaggerate so that the arms are too far away from the body. If you have to reach for the ball, the rhythmic co-ordination of the power movements of arms-wrists-hands-clubhead will be broken. Correct timing of a shot is essential. It is the link between body and clubhead. It is impossible to stipulate specific distances. Every man is a law unto himself, but you can tell by "feel" the correct distance for you. Any suggestion of having to stretch is proof that something is wrong. You must feel comfortable. That is the keynote of the three examples I have picked. Each is correct according to individual taste and feel. The photograph of Vicomtesse de Saint Sauveur has succeeded in capturing something of the essential serene, unshakeable poise that is the hall-mark of this French girl's play.

(*Opposite*) *Gary Player (South Africa)*

Peter Alliss (England)   *Vicomtesse de Saint Sauveur (France)*

11. *Left Glove Desirable*

Anything that improves a grip is important for it is the basic fundamental of the stroke. For that reason the use of a left glove is desirable. It helps to prevent the club turning in the hands at impact. Climatic conditions affect the hands, perspiring and slippery in the summer, cold in the winter. A golf glove of close-fitting leather solves such problems. It also helps the grip, enables the weaker hand to be firmer on the shaft. Be sure to use a full-fingered as opposed to the half-fingered variety or mitt. In certain cases it helps to use a right-hand glove as well.

Tony Lema (USA)

(Opposite) Arnold Palmer (USA)

12. Hands in the Takeaway

There are many theories on how the backswing is started. I visualize the movement as a co-ordination of body, arms, hands, and shaft of the club that swings the club-head back. The more fluent and natural the action, the straighter will be the line of direction. A one-piece backswing packs body-punch into the shot. Bobby Jones once said that the correct use of the hands and wrists is one of the easiest things in the world to visualize, but is about the most difficult to describe in print. This is particularly true of the start of the swing. It is simple to say that the swing begins with both hands moving to the right, the head of the club lagging behind. The advice would be sound, just as it would be timely to warn the player against lifting the club up sharply in chopper fashion or sweeping it round with a flat roll. But to concentrate on the hands and arms alone is misleading. The start of the swing is neither a turn nor a lift. It is a combination of two movements. The club is pushed back with the hands, wrists and arms. The clubhead keeps close to the ground. The left arm is straight. The right elbow is close to the side. The second motion is described in the next section. Neither movement can be ignored. Both are important. Together these initial movements virtually determine the fate of a shot.

Patrick Cros (France)   *Stan Leonard (Canada)*

Carl Poulsen (Denmark)   *Dick Meyer (USA)*

Phil Rodgers (USA)   *Beverly Hanson (USA)*

13. Hands in the Second Stage

The second motion is the turning of the left hip to the right, thus beginning the transference of weight to the right foot. The emphasis often tends to concentrate on the role of the hands and arms. Both are important, but it is fatal to forget the basic principles of correct body movement. Together they form the combination necessary for a smooth swing. This particular set of action studies of six great golfers brings out in incisive fashion the essence of the movement. There is no attempt to snatch the club up. The head does not move. The left shoulder is beginning to shift around under the chin. The wrist-cock is beginning. Although the grip is firm, it is not tense. If the club is lifted by the wrists, the club completes the backswing without the full pivot.

(a) Ben Hogan (USA)   (c) Max Faulkner (England)   (e) Lloyd Mangrum (USA)

(b) Bernard Hunt (England)   (d) Arthur Lees (England)   (f) Fred Haas (USA)

14. Hands in Stage Three

The camera has frozen the swing at an interesting stage. The act of shifting the right hip has ensured an unimpeded upswing of the hands. The pivot is not an artificial movement. It is a natural, rhythmic turn of the body. The left shoulders are pointing at the ball. The action of Ed Oliver (*b*) is of particular interest to golfers who are bulky in build. In the address his hands and arms were fairly close to the body for the practical reason that to get the pivot working, the arm extension had to be emphasized. Correct timing is largely dependent on muscular co-ordination. Many rotund golfers fail to realize that lack of suppleness and this co-ordination are responsible for faults creeping into their game. Oliver was as fit as an ox. Nobody could fault his muscular co-ordination. Even so, his bulk made certain modifications necessary in his swing. In the backswing his hands at the top were roughly shoulder-high. I have included action studies of two of Britain's brightest young golfers, Ronnie Shade (*f*) and Clive Clark (*d*), both polished strikers of the ball.

(*a*) *Doug Sanders (USA)*   (*c*) *Willie Turnesa (USA)*   (*e*) *Harry Weetman (England)*

(*b*) *Ed Oliver (USA)*   (*d*) *Clive Clark (England)*   (*f*) *Ronnie Shade (Scotland)*

c

d

45

f

15. Hands that Ignored Logic

In James Bruen we had an amateur capable of winning the Amateur and Open titles on both sides of the Atlantic had he taken the trouble to work at his game. I watched him win the Boys' Championship at Birkdale, crushing Innes in the final by 11 and 9. In the Walker Cup trials at St. Andrews his first round was 68. The next three cards beat Bobby Jones's record by 2 shots. In nine rounds he only once needed more than 71. He won the Amateur at Birkdale in 1946, beating Bobby Sweeny 4 and 3. His golf was not as impressive. The ball was driven prodigious distances, but the willow scrub took its toll, including three smashed clubs.

These action studies illustrate his unique method of hitting a golf ball. Few could imitate his style to advantage. The famous "loop" at the top of the backswing with the right arm well away from the body and hands high contradicts orthodox teaching, yet the idiosyncrasy is ironed out during the downswing, and the ball struck firm, square, straight and far. He had a very firm grip of the club, whilst his shoulders were exceptionally supple. It is interesting to copy the "loop" and see what happens.

16. Hands that Overcame Physical Disability

It is by no means true that the major personalities of golf are the most interesting. Indeed, in a sense, the opposite is true. Those who take the leading roles are often so obvious that there is really nothing to say about them. Ed Furgol does not come in that category. Here is a man who not only overcame a physical disability that could so easily have ruled out golf, but so adapted his game that even a withered and locked left arm was able to play an active part in his swing. His shot-making silences the advocates of a straight left arm. Such was his skill that rounds of 71, 70, 71, 72 gave him a winning aggregate of 284 in the most prized title in American professional golf, the U.S. Open Championship, in 1954. It is interesting to watch him in action on the links. His face is immovably serene, but it cannot, however grimly he purses his lips and fiercely knits his eyebrows, assume the lineaments of total agony. He lacks the tragic mask. At the most dramatic crisis, his face assumes a self-conscious, almost boyish grin. He has at his command a deadly ironic urbanity tinged with an attractive American drawl. It is interesting to study the hands, wrists and arms of the man who has achieved the impossible against the most formidable golfing opposition in the world.

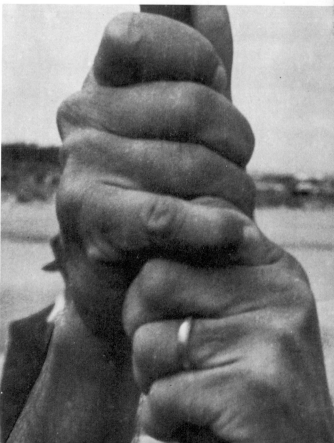

(a) *Frank Stranahan (USA)*

(b) *Tom Haliburton (Scotland)*

17. Wrists at Top of Backswing

This is one of the most vital parts of the swing. What happens here determines whether the shot will be successful or not. The secret to good golf could be here, but so many golfers ignore the fact. Elementary check-points are that at the top of the backswing the wrists must be cocked and the grip firm. Any golfer will tell you such advice is kid stuff. Maybe so. The same criticism might be levelled should I add that if the club is allowed to drop below the horizontal, the chances are that the wrist-cocking will be out of control, the grip will be relaxed, and the shaft will be held by the finger-tips. This is stale advice, but the fact remains that many golfers ignore it. The feel of such a grip can be deceptive. It suggests a freedom of movement that has no value. In the downswing the grip is altered. At impact the grip, the club having turned in the hands, is different from what it was at the address. An easy way to check whether this is a weakness—set the driver in an address position after playing a shot. If the grip has to be modified, it suggests that the fingers have let go. Some players prefer to use a three-quarter swing under complete control rather than risk

a flamboyant back-sweep that looks good but is unpredictable at impact. If you position yourself at the back of the tee during a tournament, look for the left-hand grip at the top of the backswing and note how firm are the three fingers on view as they hold the shaft.

Another fault with long-handicap golfers is to let the arms go away from the body when the downswing begins. The result at impact is that the clubhead strikes the ball from the outside, cutting across into a slice. What players must remember is that the left wrist should be underneath the shaft at the top of the backswing. When the downswing begins, the left hand starts the "pulling-down" movement with the arms kept into the body. Another fault is the tendency to bend the left wrist outwards at the top of the backswing. The movement "shuts" the clubface and invites a sharp hook.

(c) *Norman Sutton* (*England*)

Such pointers can be studied in these frozen action studies of twelve great professionals: Frank Stranahan (*a*) looks like a caricature of physical perfection—at that time he had the perfect frame for golf; Tom Haliburton (*b*) was a methodical stylist with an impeccable swing; Norman Sutton (*c*), member of a famous golfing family, had a neat, workmanlike style; Mike Souchak (*d*), huge, enthusiastic, voice juicy and measured, had no loose ends of personality, but was a shade dogmatic—but then who is not on the American tournament trail? Four names with shining records in American championship history: Gene Littler (*e*), Clayton Heafner (*f*), Bill Collins (*g*) and Billy Casper (*h*); Britain's Jack Hargreaves (*i*), with the strong, almost peasant hands; Jerry Barber (*j*), who skippered the U.S. Ryder Cup side at Lindrick, a somewhat misleading man with a wrinkled face the colour of alabaster worn smooth by the years and a smile like a benevolent winch, his golf is that of a sprightly young man; Jay Herbert (*k*), personification of American sophistication; and the incomparable Ben Hogan (*l*). These are twelve men whose styles repay close, analytical study.

(d) Mike Souchak (USA)   *(e) Gene Littler (USA)*

(f) Clayton Heafner (USA)   *(g) Bill Collins (USA)*

(h) Billy Casper (USA)   *(i) Jack Hargreaves (England)*

(j) Jerry Barber (USA)   *(k) Jay Herbert (USA)*   *(l) Ben Hogan (USA)*

18. Gary Player in Action

In an age in which would-be champions are plentiful and champions are rare, Gary Player occupies a unique place in contemporary golf. Although Bobby Jones and Ben Hogan are his superiors as stylists, whilst one or two others might rank alongside him on the same score, Player stands out in unmistakable fashion. His record speaks for itself. He is the only playing professional in the world to have won the four premier titles of the United States and British Opens, the Masters, and the American P.G.A. Championship. Add to these the Canada Cup for South Africa with Harold Henning as partner in Madrid, and the premier professional match-play event of the world at Wentworth in 1965, when in the semi-final he beat Tony Lema after trailing 7 down with 17 to play. This incredible bag of titles has been gained by the age of twenty-nine. He is in the Hogan class, the gold standard of golf.

It will be interesting to see what happens now that some of the keen edge of ambition has worn itself off. He has achieved both influence and status. The anxious man inside has begun to relax. Off the fairways, professional golfers are too often boring. Player is an exception. Perhaps the nicest tribute that can be paid to the South African is the fondness which people in and behind the scenes have for him, and this is acquired without any effort on his part, for his personality does not project in forms of extroverted *bonhomie*. It is simply that anyone who comes to know Player, even the caddies, who can become very blasé about their men, acquires such affection and respect for his integrity and seriousness of purpose that through no conscious effort on his part, he finds himself surrounded by admirers. Undoubtedly a great personality in a sport not too richly endowed with outstanding men.

The temptation to isolate the secret of Player's success is always real. He alone knows the answer, but from observation it would seem that systematic building-up of physical strength has been a major contributory factor. I recall a conversation with him in the Adelphi Hotel, Liverpool, in 1956. The Open was being staged at Hoylake; the winner, Peter Thomson, taking the title with an aggregate of 286. Player was 4th with 291. He compared his style with Hogan's, analysed Thomson's methods, and wound up by confessing that his main worry was lack of length. Unless he could add some 30 yards to his drives, the initial advantage went to his opponents. Comparisons of length are easily made. For a long time Thomson could out-drive the little South African, but the Wentworth match-play final in 1965 provided two rounds of stroke-by-stroke checking. This time Player out-drove his opponent with ease.

Note the careful placement of hands on the shaft. In essence a natural grip with both arms extended.

This triple sequence gives some indication of the way the hands and wrists lash the clubhead into and through the ball.

There is no attempt to slow-up at the finish. Tremendous leverage, beautiful balance, exceptionally strong grip. It is still firm, although the momentum of the club has brought the body round.

The improvement had not happened by chance. Systematic and determined exercises have brought Player's body to the peak of physical perfection. No longer is he the puny little golfer, but a pocket Hercules capable of more than holding his own against the most powerful players. When he hits a ball, every part of his body plays its part. What most impressed me was the increased strength in his hands. I regard Player's grip as wellnigh perfect. Unquestionably the intensive exercises have helped. Every day he does about seventy finger-tip push-ups. Over a period of time his hands, wrists, arms and shoulders have strengthened beyond recognition. Add to these the deep knee-bends that have toned up his legs, and a variation—the slow knee-bend and stretch executed with his wife on his back. Player claims that eighteen months of this exercise put $1\frac{1}{2}$ inches on his thigh-muscle girth:

sit-up exercises have developed his stomach muscles. In short, Player is in magnificent physical shape.

   This form of muscular improvement is available to anyone who has the patience and determination to work systematically at such exercises. It must be done gradually. Over-enthusiasm can only lead to strained muscles. A simple beginning is to splay the fingers and press down with full force for about ten seconds. Repeat about a dozen times. Gradually your fingers, forearms and wrists will get stronger. Do not forget that with the average right-hander, the left hand is the one that needs extra attention. It is just that much weaker. A supplementary exercise is squeezing a small rubber ball about a dozen times with each hand, repeating it whenever possible. The long-term benefit of this simple exercise is marked. I had first-hand experience of its value in another sport. Richie Ginther, the Californian Grand Prix driver, was testing a B.R.M. on our private track when without warning it spun off and burst into flames. Fortunately the accident occurred by the pit. A mechanic rolled the driver, who was on fire, in his coat, and he was rushed to hospital, badly burned. The injuries included both hands. During convalescence, it was feared that gripping strength had been affected. The muscles needed building up. Two-handed drill with a rubber ball was introduced. In spite of the pain, Ginther persevered. Every time I saw him the fingers were kneading away. It paid dividends. Two months later he drove in the Monaco Grand Prix with hands and muscles as good as ever. Golfers can add strength to their fingers and wrists if only they will take Gary Player's dedicated quest for physical fitness to heart. The exercises are there, in essence, simplicity itself. All they require is perseverance. The final result is bound to produce maximum power in your swing.

Gary Player's putting style is compact, comfortable and workmanlike. Hands and arms are close to the body. Note position of right thumb on the shaft.

(a) "Chick" Harbert (USA)

19. *How Far Back?*

There can be no set ruling as to how far the club should be taken back. There will always be extremes. On the other hand, I can safely say that to take the club beyond the horizontal is to skirt trouble. It makes it more difficult to register maximum club-head speed at impact. The player hits too early. There is always the possibility of loosening the grip—a fault that completely upsets a shot. The clubhead must come squarely into the ball. The hands regain their firmness in the downswing, but nine times out of ten the damage has been done. Many hooks, slices and sockets are due to the temptation to take the club beyond the horizontal. There are some players, however, whose body suppleness allows them to take exceptionally long backswings. Not only do they need this full sweep for maximum power, but it is also under strict control. I have chosen three such men to illustrate this group: "Chick" Harbert (*a*), the American with superb physique and prodigious driving power; Harry Weetman (*c*), one of the longest and straightest drivers in Britain; and Geoffrey Hunt (*b*), who can belt the ball indecent distances. It is also interesting to compare the full sweep of Adams (*e*) with the more curtailed action of Gregson (*d*), and the moderate back-swing of Hitchcock (*f*), Waltman (*g*) and Casper (*h*). Inevitably you pays your money and you takes your choice.

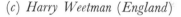

(*b*) *Geoffrey Hunt (England)*   (*c*) *Harry Weetman (England)*

(d) *Malcolm Gregson* (*England*)

(e) *Jimmy Adams* (*Scotland*)

(f) *Jimmy Hitchcock* (*England*)

(g) *Retief Waltman* (*South Africa*)

(h) *Billy Casper* (*USA*)

20. A Backswing that might be Dangerous

Although I stress the importance of a firm grip with the last three fingers of the left hand at the top of the backswing—that if the grip loosens, the downswing is thrown out of joint, even though the hands reassert their firmness, that here is a potential cause of hooks, slices, sockets, and so on—I include this action study of Cecil Ewing to prove that there are always exceptions to a rule. This burly Irish Walker Cup player appears to have slackened his left hand grip completely, yet honesty compels me to admit that the shot in question would do justice to Player or Nicklaus. On the other hand, I do not recommend its adoption by an average player unless he is anxious to explore lesser frequented parts of the course.

(a) *Peter Thomson* (*Australia*)

(b) *David Thomas* (*Wales*)

21. Straight or Bent?

Harry Vardon contended that it was impossible for the left arm to be straight at the point of the swing where so many golfers believed it to be. Maybe it was wishful thinking, for Vardon's left arm was very bent. One thing is certain. Good golf can be played with the left arm straight or bent. I have chosen two examples of each—and all four men have brilliant shot-making records. The trouble is that some golfers who plump for the straight left arm theory find they have substituted rigidity, which is tantamount to playing golf in a strait-jacket. Many golfers are not physically built to imitate David Thomas (*b*). Far better to use a modified version of Tolley's (*d*) majestic style, and probably at the same time ease the difficulty of keeping firm those last three fingers of the left hand on the grip at the top of the backswing.

(*d*) *Cyril Tolley* (*England*)

(*c*) *Brian Huggett* (*Wales*)

22. *Three Champions in Action*   (I) TONY LEMA

Tony Lema is not an easy man to paint in an accurate pen-portrait. Like Cyrano de Bergerac, the secret of his appeal lies in the fact that everything about him is somehow out of focus. The edges are blurred. He has an abrupt manner and austerity of precept, plus a characteristic American combination of shrewdness and generosity. Under pressure his face becomes as unalterable as one of Euclid's axioms. At times he is glacial rather than genial. Sometimes he gives the impression that the end of the world when it comes will surely be announced with an American accent. Judging by the signs of the times it could well be so. On the other hand, in relaxed mood many rounds are enlivened by the authentic echoes of his salty conversation. He talks graphically in a quiet toneless nasal voice. His rare golfing ability was generally recognized at an early stage, and I am sure never seriously doubted by himself when he compared it with others. He has an enormous belief in himself. At times he can be as calculating as a slot machine. Newspapers, radio and television have given considerable space to his many successes, but I have a feeling that what really counts is that certain people he respects now take him seriously. He has accepted the fact that supreme golfing honours have come his way, but there is no visible arrogance in him, no mock modesty. His ability is great, his application monumental. Three action studies yield little of a man's game, but in the light of what is written elsewhere they show several interesting points, if only by comparison.

Although slim in build, Charles has exceptionally strong hands, wrists and forearms. In the address it would be possible to draw a straight line from the right shoulder down the arm and shaft to the clubhead. At impact note the left-hand knuckles, forefinger and thumb. The grip might have been moulded on the shaft.

(II) BOB CHARLES

Many left-handed golfers are aggrieved. They claim that the topography of golf courses is against them, maintaining that they are laid out specifically for the right-handed player. It is an interesting thought. The majority of golf architects are right-handed gentlemen and the average course is laid out with a view to play by right-handers, but closer examination shows there are arguments for both sides. A well-hit shot in the right direction gets its true reward be the player right- or left-handed, though a right-hander might argue that the traps meant to penalize an indifferent tee shot frequently catch the slice rather than the hook, which, of course, corresponds to the left-hander's slice. Sidehill lies usually even out. Most greens are designed so that a carefully placed shot, whether to right or left, will find the target.

Another complaint is the poor choice of clubs. I am not in a position to argue this point, but it is a grumble often heard. Another growl is more common. There are professionals who argue that no man can play good golf left-handed. Such an attitude assumes that man is naturally a creature of instinctive right-handed habits. This argument extends to those who insist that a child with a natural left-handed tendency must transfer his urge to the right hand. I question whether this is for the eventual good of the child. To change from the left hand, which in certain cases was obviously designed by nature as the master-hand, to the right, puts the individual in question at a disadvantage. He is neither left-handed nor right-handed.

But Hagen, Jones, Sweetser and Aubrey Boomer were naturally left-handed, though they played right-handed golf. There is no reason why a player must be mediocre just because he is ambidextrous.

The argument that no left-hander had ever won a major tournament or championship was debunked by such eminent southpaws as Ivor Thomas, P. B. Lucas, Len Nettlefold, and more recently Bob Charles, who won the 1963 British Open at Royal Lytham and St. Annes. The New Zealander has powerful but sensitive hands. Few golfers seem to have such controlled clubhead speed. Throughout the swing the grip is firm. Impact finds the hands in the same position as at the address. The way his hands take the clubhead through the ball is an object lesson on how the speed of the swing can be regulated.

A most convincing putting style. There is no hint of tension or over-tightening of the forearm muscles. The New Zealander is an incomparable holer-out.

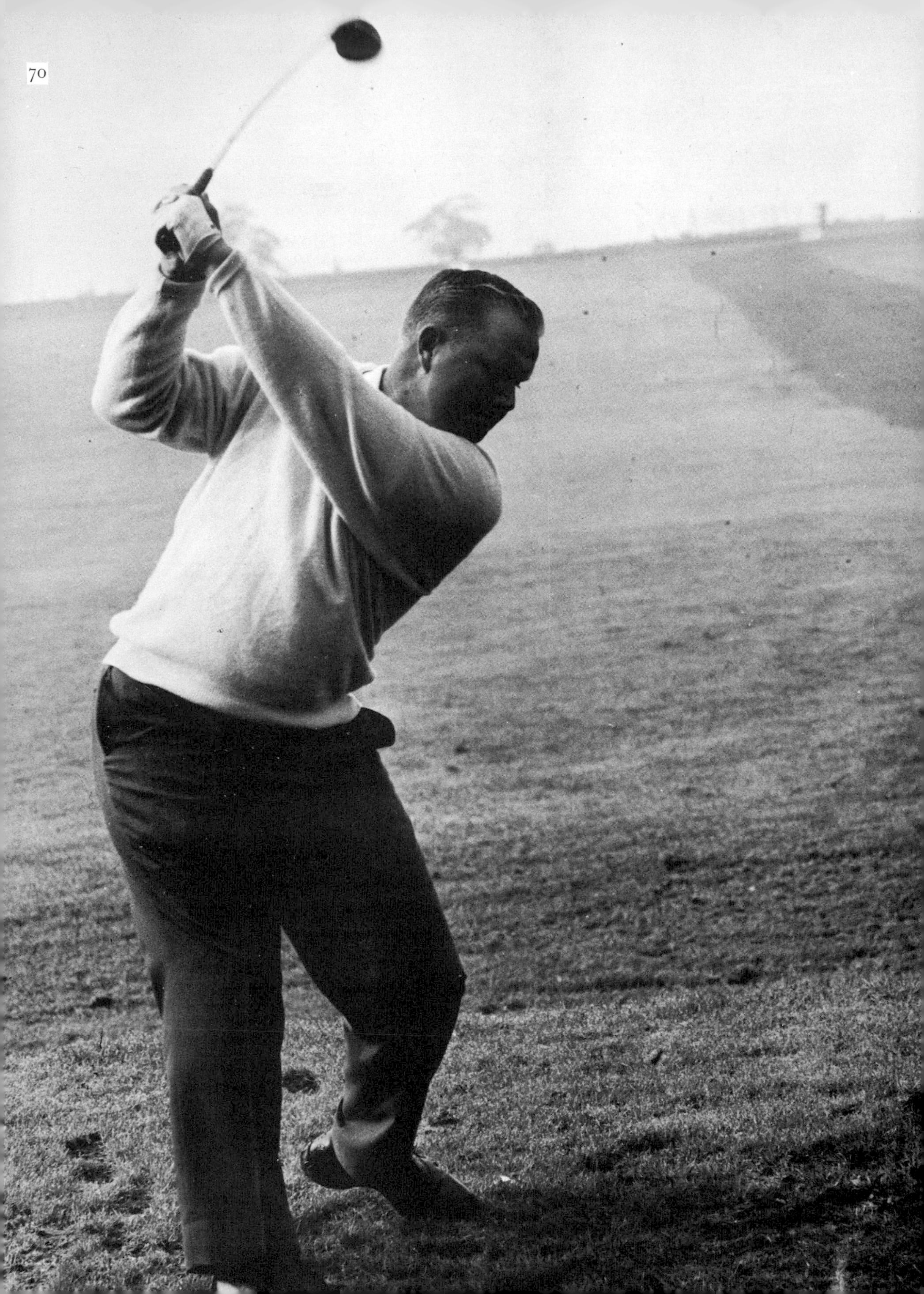

(III) JACK NICKLAUS

In appearance Jack Nicklaus is a muscular, beefy, butcher-looking man with a face like Mickey Rooney. At times he looks pugnacious, but underneath he has a nature that can also be simple and forthright. Despite his somewhat rustic appearance, he has a presence, an air of distinction. When bored with company or conversation, a vague smile is painted on his face while his mind is on other things. On occasions it is possible to reach out for the ultimate word in the dictionary of appraisal and find him "great". About a fifth of his golfing skill is a composite of grit and determination. The rest is pure genius, something that is rarer than gold. Regarding his style, I look upon Nicklaus as an ideal player on whom to base one's game, provided you have similar build and stature. As in the case of Tony Lema, I am not going to draw conclusions from the visual evidence of his swing. Instead I recommend these action studies as rich material to study, analyse and compare with the rest of the world's finest players.

Gary Player (South Africa)

Johnny Bulla (USA)

23. *Last Three Fingers of the Left Hand*

The golf grip is basically a problem of pressures. The hands are often the weakest part of a long-handicap golfer's game, particularly in iron play. Impact comes before the clubhead has reached the lowest point of the arc of the swing. The ball leaves the ground like a bullet with a low boring trajectory. An average golfer playing the same shot scoops the ball into the air with little carry, the shot entirely at the mercy of any hostile wind. The fault is due to weak hands. A golfer is only as good as his hands. The fingers apply the pressure; they also experience the "feel" of the club. There must be the firmness of control without the loosening of hands at the top of the backswing. At this point the last three fingers of the left hand determine whether the shot to be played is going to be accurate or otherwise. Study these four action studies very carefully. Look at each left hand. That hand has the task of keeping the club-head in the correct position throughout the swing. You can tell if the right side has usurped control by the tendency to hit from the top. The danger-sign is unmistakable. A firm left-hand grip on the club is essential. Loosening the last three fingers at the top undermines the entire structure of the swing. If you find it difficult, try shortening the backswing.

Phil Rodgers (USA)   *Doug Sanders (USA)*

a

b

c

d

24. Shut or Open?

There is plenty of talk about the shut-face method, but many golfers are somewhat woolly-minded as to what it is all about. Shut-face means that the clubface at the top of the backswing looks at the sky instead of the toe pointing to the ground. The best way to describe it is by visual comparison. With this method goes the shut-face grip in which all four knuckles on the left hand are on view at the address. The photograph of Claude Harmon (e) caused Henry Cotton to say it was the "shuttest" shut-face he had ever seen. That opinion was not exaggerated. I know of no other player in first-class golf with such a phenomenal action. The reason is not hard to find. I doubt if many players are strong enough to withstand the strain imposed by this left-wrist action and interlocking grip. The best way is to try it out. Not everyone will be able to swing the club into the position shown here. Even if they succeed, not many will manage to bring the club down so that at impact it is square to the ball. You may be the exception, but few golfers could use this action with all the shots in the game. The strain is too great. The effect of such a shut-faced action is to keep the ball low. But it reduces the range of shots. Cut-up pitch and fade are ruled out. Not only that, but the margin between success and failure is very narrow. On the whole this action does not commend itself to indiscriminate copying. It suits Harmon. It might well be adapted by others of like build and physique, but it is too exacting for the average golfer.

(a) *Douglas Ford (USA)*

(b) *Reginald Whitcombe (England)*

(c) *Norman Sutton (England)*

(d) *Eric Lester (England)*

(e) *Claude Harmon (USA)*

e

25. *Left Arm and Wrist in the Downpull*

To all intents and purposes the left hand plays an unobtrusive part in the swing. Power is infused by the right hand. Nevertheless the left hand has a vital contribution to make. Not only is the club taken to the top of the backswing with the left hand in control, but the first stages of the downswing are under left-hand guidance. These three action studies illustrate the pulling action of left shoulder, arm and hand. The photograph of Tommy Bolt (*left*) is particularly instructive on this point. You can almost feel the downward pull. Bolt is one of the "characters" of American golf. Some years ago a bad patch in a tournament would invoke arms windmilling, possibly clubs flying. He gave the impression of being possessed by an adhesive demon that was fiercely resisting exorcism. But he is good value. There are far too few of this type about today. Reverting to this question of left-hand lead, most of the troubles at impact are caused by the right hand taking charge too soon. The answer is to become left hand conscious. Although it will be difficult at first, try swinging and then hitting with the left hand only.

(*Opposite*) *Tommy Bolt* (*USA*)

Eric Brown (*Scotland*)   *S. W. T. Murray* (*Scotland*)

26. Arnold Palmer in Action

It is difficult to describe Arnold Palmer in a few words. He is a curious mixture of extremes. Nothing perturbs him. His face has the anonymity of granite. Being a reasonably immodest man, he saw himself early on as one of the world's greatest golfers. Of course, so do many others, but in Palmer's case it came true. So many words have been written about him, yet he would only be human if every additional adulatory word reinforced the terror ordinary people would feel at the thought of having to face the galleries again and measure up to the legend, for a legend he has become in his own lifetime, and legends are the best part of the golfing world. He has

a dry sense of humour—sometimes funnier than he realizes. He can be relaxed and entertaining, particularly when his attractive wife is present. She has a happy knack of stifling any attempt at an *ex cathedra* delivery on the part of her husband. On the course Palmer has more panache than many of his colleagues, is unruffled under pressure, and plays literally every shot in the bag with complete control and sympathetic understanding. I have gathered together a sequence of this champion in action. The shots reflect an accurate picture of his style. It is all there for the reader to study. I prefer it to be action without words. The very strokes are expressive in themselves. As in the other style studies of Lema and Nicklaus, a tremendous amount can be assimilated by analysis and comparison.

Arnold Palmer (USA)

Arnold Palmer (USA)

Neil Coles (England)

Guy Wolstenholme (England)

27. Right Wrist-cock and Weight Shift

This series of action studies show how the clubhead is behind the hands in the downswing. There lies the secret of clubhead acceleration. The uncoiling of hands, arms and body, the uncocking of the wrists, and transfer of weight to the left foot: all part of a rhythmic movement that gathers momentum until the moment of impact. To be sure of uncocking the right wrist at the right moment, the left arm pulls the club down, and being straight ensures that the right arm comes in to the side. The moment that happens is the split-second to begin the uncocking process. The right arm will straighten out as can be seen in the Demaret photograph until at impact it will resemble the address position, only this time it will be at maximum clubhead speed.

Flory van Donck (Belgium)   *Jimmy Demaret (USA)*

(a) Peter Butler (England)

(b) Lawson Little (USA)

(c) Kel Nagle (Australia)

28. Right Elbow into Side

Here are five examples of how the right elbow should be tucked in at this point of the swing. It would be difficult to find better instances. Between good and great golfers is fixed a great gulf which is crossed only by the elect. There are no doubts about these men's qualifications. Between them they combine tremendous power in the long game with delicacy of touch around the greens. Look in particular at Lawson Little (*b*), the American who finished 12 up at the end of the first round of the 1934 British Amateur final and went on to win 14 up and 13. The majestic Bobby Locke (*d*), resolute Kel Nagle (*c*), stylist Peter Butler (*a*) and immaculate Arnold Palmer (*e*)—all have this vital factor in common, the right elbow in close to the body. That is one feature that every golfer can copy to advantage. In this way you hit the ball with an inside-out swing, a method that pays dividends in accuracy and distance.

(*d*) *Bobby Locke (South Africa)*   (*e*) *Arnold Palmer (USA)*

Ben Arda (Philippines)

29. *Pulling Down with the Left Hand*

The pulling action of the left shoulder and arm is evident in all three action studies—you can almost feel the muscular reaction. The left hand takes a firm grip for it serves as a positional check of clubhead position during the swing. That does not mean an over-tense grip, a mistake which leads to over-taut muscles. A feature about Ben Arda's backswing (*left*) is the smooth, rhythmic co-ordination by club and hands. The movement is started by the hands rather than the clubhead, a tip that gives width to the swing. The best advice to give to an average golfer about the start of the downswing is that he should confine himself to the positive thought that it is the left arm and hand that are in control at this juncture. They are responsible for the pulling-down action until the left hand comes level with the right hip.

Mario Gonzalez (Brazil)   *Otto Schoepfer (Switzerland)*

30. Perfect Co-ordination and Timing

When Henry Cotton announced that he had played in his last Open Championship, we lost one of the few colourful personalities in British golf. There is no one else quite like him. His voice has a dry mundane metropolitan quality. During play his face can be so steely that not even a flicker of an eyelash would betray a royal flush if he were engaged at poker with his life at stake. Few golfers have ever subjected themselves to such ice-cold concentrated self-discipline. In my opinion he is the finest striker of a golf ball in Britain. In this action study (*a*) there is perfect co-ordination of arms and hands as the wrists are about to uncoil.

Charles Ward (*b*) is a smaller man than many of his colleagues, but unquestionably a better golfer. This action study taken when the little professional was at his prime is interesting when compared with Cotton. The latter's hands have arrived at a point in the downswing almost opposite the ball, but his wrists are still bent back. The clubhead has to move through an arc of several feet compared with the few inches shift of the hands before the moment of impact. In Ward's case that acceleration of clubhead speed has taken place, which gives some idea of the force generated when the right hand steps up the action.

(*Right*) *Charles Ward* (*England*)

(*Opposite*) *Henry Cotton* (*England*)

Gary Player (South Africa)

Tony Lema (USA)

31. *Split-second before Maximum Speed*

As the club enters the hitting area, the right elbow is well in to the side preparatory to straightening. The left side moves out of the way. The clubhead speed is accelerated through the uncocking of the wrists, a movement that takes place when the hands have reached a point below the waist-line. The action is almost too fast for the onlooker to take in the details. It is possible, though, to note the terrific thrust developed by the right side, and the way the right arm moves in to the side as the left side prepares to take the full power of the drive. The shifting of the left hip out of the way is to allow the hands to flow through without interruption. The head is well anchored. A common fault with the long-handicap player is to uncock the wrists too early in the downswing. The right hand takes command far too soon. The result is that the power has gone out of the shot before impact. The first stage of the downswing must have definite left-hand guidance. At the top of the backswing, the position is that of a coiled spring. The potential is there. Only when the club enters the hitting area is the power unleashed. At this point clubhead acceleration speed is terrific. The right forearm injects the force into the drive as the wrists lash the clubhead into the ball. Very often the folds of the trousers indicate something of the dynamism infused into the shot.

Sam Snead (USA)   *Smiley Quick (USA)*

Max Faulkner (England)

32. Wrists and Hitting Late

These action studies show three perfect hitting positions. Reproduce such a swing and your shot-making would be as crisp as any professional, but to get proper results everything depends on the question of wrist-strength. That is the snag of the late hit. The phrase is used glibly by golfers, often without appreciating exactly what it means. Holding the wrist-break in the downswing until the hands are literally opposite the ball is reasonably simple, but to whip the club through so that the face is square to the ball at impact requires wrist-strength that many golfers do not possess. Many players hit far too late. The full force of clubhead acceleration comes into play after impact. The result is a snatched half-hit shot. It is better to get the left arm and club in the approved straight line a split-second before impact than to ruin the shot by misjudging the moment to apply maximum pressure. Strengthening the wrists, fingers and forearms with systematic exercises helps to make hitting late a practical possibility.

Jimmy Hitchcock (England)   *Dai Rees (Wales)*

33. Copybook Grip, but up on the Toes

On the average a golf swing needs two seconds to complete. The backswing accounts for more than a second. Acceleration comes at the most revealing point, the hitting area. It is a closed zone to the majority of players. Few know what they do or look like at this stage. These action studies are informative. What they reveal runs counter to the adage that the left heel must be firmly anchored to the ground at the moment of impact. In each instance both heels are in mid-air at the psychological moment. The cause invites speculation. The mannerism may well be a subconscious counter to the pull of the swing. Many golfers who rise up on their toes at this juncture of the swing are unaware of the fact. The resistance to the force of the swing is quite unconscious. It must therefore be regarded as an essential part of some players' game, disastrous in theory, effective in practice, but dangerous to copy.

(*Opposite*) *Willie Turnesa (USA)*

Jacqueline Gordon (England)   *Zara Bolton (Ireland)*

Bobby Locke (South Africa)

Jerry Barber (USA)

34. Controlled Right-hand Thrust

Some professionals say that it is not essential for the right elbow to be tucked in close to the body during the backswing, maintaining that the most natural position for it is pointing to the ground and slightly away from the side. This advice runs counter to the old test of tucking a handkerchief under the right armpit. If it drops before impact there is room for improvement in the style. These contradictory assertions prove once again that it is unwise to dogmatize in golf. Actually it is possible to confirm both views. Those who possess a pronounced flat swing can pass the handkerchief test with ease, for the right elbow automatically hugs the side. To apply the same methods to an upright swing is asking for trouble. Over-concentration upon the maxim "tuck that right elbow in" cramps the style, a fault as troublesome as the other extreme of sticking the right elbow out at right angles. Bobby Locke's position (*left*) is wellnigh flawless. The entire action personifies distribution of weight, balance and force under complete control. The position of the right elbow in all four examples is ideal—controlled without being cramped.

Dai Rees (Wales)   *Ian Caldwell (England)*

35. *Hands Ahead of Ball*

The movement of the swing at this stage of a shot is too fast for the naked eye, but it can be confirmed by high-speed photography. This particular action divides the thoroughbred from the selling-plater. If your hands lag behind the clubhead at impact, you are going to produce a powder-puff shot, a feeble lofted effort without power. It does not happen by chance. Practice alone will enable you to master the art of getting the hands ahead of the ball just before impact. Ronnie White (*a*) knew precisely the position of his hands in relation to the clubhead at this point of the shot. He was one of our greatest amateurs. He possessed the mental and physical qualities of Hogan or Player. Confidence and concentration were stamped on his shots, whilst his greenwork was an object-lesson in delicacy of touch. This action study, plus those of Burton (*c*), Miguel (*b*) and Morey (*d*), demonstrate what I mean by hitting through the ball with controlled power. Practice will produce this knack, but only if a deliberate attempt is made to "feel" your hands ahead of the ball just before impact.

(*Opposite*) *Ronnie White* (*England*)

(*b*) *Angel Miguel* (*Spain*)   (*c*) *Dick Burton* (*England*)   (*d*) *Dale Morey* (*USA*)

36. Left Arm and Hand at Impact

At impact the verdict is favourable when shaft and left arm form a straight line. The position is almost identical with the address. In both cases the clubhead has flowed in a line parallel to the line of flight. The left arm is taking the hit. After the club entered the hitting area, the wrists uncocked, and right hand and arm infused power into the shot, but did not overpower the left hand, arm and side. The body was braced to take the strain. Everyone is always looking for extra yards, and there are aids for forcing shots such as a longer backswing, more pronounced pivot, or wider stance, but all are valueless without this increased clubhead acceleration in the hitting area. There is one snag. Every player has a natural maximum clubhead speed. Beyond that it is not safe to go. The two men I have chosen to emphasize these points are names that have enriched golfing history. Many years of international golf have

conferred stature of rare significance on Francis Ouimet, though full appreciation of his skill is in proportion to one's knowledge of the game. In a way his appearance epitomized his methods. Both were elegant, urbane and disciplined. Ouimet did not invent any new style. There was nothing of the flamboyance of Walter Hagen or the intensity of Henry Cotton. He simply manicured it. He brought finesse to the sport. Fred Daly is a complete contrast. He has a cocky, Irish charm. He could commit murder and still persuade people it was not his fault. There was always a jaunty air about his golf that could be misleading. His attitude was carefree, but the shots were devastating in their accuracy.

(Opposite) Francis Ouimet (USA)

(Right) Fred Daly (Ireland)

37. Right Shoulder, Elbow and Hand at Impact

Here are three perfect action shots of this particular angle of a stroke. They show at a glance how body power co-ordinates with the role played by the hands. The tucking-in of the right elbow ensures that the full force of the shot is generated and transmitted through the hands. It is also a safeguard against the left hand being overpowered by the right. At this point of the swing the acceleration of clubhead speed is terrific. Note and compare the position of the right hand and the angle of the left arm. Roberto de Vicenzo (*b*) has been a frequent invader to these shores, twice almost winning the Open title. He never alters, shrugs incessantly, radiates mildness, has a vice-like hand-grip, disarms the stiffest critics with a broad grin, has a philosophical habit of accepting defeat and a cigarette with the same air of inevitability. Dick Meyer (*c*) is always worth watching. This former American Open champion possesses a classic style that never gets out of joint. He has a keen sense of humour and is blessed with an even temper. Retief Waltman (*a*) has tremendous potential and works at his game with all the enthusiasm of youth.

(*Opposite*) *Retief Waltman (South Africa)*

(*b*) *Roberto de Vicenzo (Argentine)*   (*c*) *Dick Meyer (USA)*

38. Hand Placement Right, Clubface Square at Impact

The actual grip used is a matter of individual preference, ranging from overlapping, interlocking palm, and two-handed like a cricket grip. But, whichever grip is used, it is essentially a two-handed affair. The left supplies control, the right infuses power, both so co-ordinated that they work together as one. The golf swing is essentially one movement inspired by a single mechanism. To make that possible, correct hand placement is essential. Equally important is the necessity of bringing the clubface at impact square to the line of flight. Study these action studies of Bruce Crampton (*a*), Phil Rodgers (*c*) and Ronnie White (*b*). Words are unnecessary. It is all there to see. Correct hand placement, and clubface square at impact, together solve ninety per cent of golfing headaches.

(*Opposite*) *Bruce Crampton (Australia)*

(*b*) *Ronnie White (England)*　　　　　(*c*) *Phil Rodgers (USA)*

a

b

c

39. The Cycle of Wrist Acceleration

This series of photographs emphasize how in the last quarter of the swing before impact the right hand takes over. The action of the left arm with its pulling-down movement brings the right arm into the correct hitting position. The right elbow is brought into the side, the wrists are cocked. Both Ford (*a*) and Sanders (*c*) show the degree of tension felt in the left arm, but as the thrust of the right forearm and hand step up the acceleration, so the right arm straightens, and the right wrist-cock is released. The transference of roles is so rhythmically achieved that in a sound shot only the camera can isolate the moment of transition. The photograph of Joe Carr (*e*) is a perfect example of hand and wrist position a split-second after impact. An appreciative onlooker is Alex Kyle, the former British Amateur champion.

(*a*) *Douglas Ford (USA)*

(*b*) *Billy Casper (USA)*   (*d*) *Beverly Hanson (USA)*

(*c*) *Doug Sanders (USA)*   (*e*) *Joe Carr (Ireland)*

(a) Henry Cotton (England)   (c) George Will (Scotland)   (e) Fred Haas (USA)

(b) Francis Smith (England)   (d) George Will (Scotland)   (f) Peter Alliss (England)

40. Hands and Clubhead at Address and Impact

The action studies in this book have been subjected to analytical treatment. Individual characteristics are there for all the world to see. Diversity of interpretation is inevitable. No two golfing styles are identical. Each of these golfers has idiosyncrasies as distinctive as his finger-prints. On the other hand, certain fundamentals are common to all. One of these is that impact-position is almost identical with the address. The eight examples confirm this fact. The angle taken of the George Will (*c* and *d*) shots is perhaps the most convincing, but Fred Haas (*e*) and Peter Alliss (*f*) make a good pair. If anyone wants to copy a perfectly balanced stance, he could do no better than base his game on Henry Cotton (*a*) as he addresses the ball in the Open Championship at Hoylake. Cotton has the knack of making everything about the golf swing look simple, easy and fluent. The same applies to the others, but somehow to me Henry Cotton always has an authoritative air about his shot-making. It has stood him in good stead throughout his playing career.

(*g*) *Phil Rodgers (USA)*   (*h*) *Hsieh Yung-Yo (China)*

41. Ken Venturi in Action

Venturi's golfing career has been one of extremes. Between 1957 and 1960 he won ten P.G.A. tournaments, and twice narrowly missed the Masters. Then came a slump. Three years passed without a single win. Stake-money dwindled to next to nothing. The primary cause was a damaged nerve in his back that almost paralysed his right side. Rejoining the tournament circuit, he found his fluent swing had gone. He could not get his right hand up in the backswing. Modifications did not work. It looked as if a brilliant playing career had ended. Analysis of his swing showed a tendency to steer the ball instead of swinging through. With patience and determination Venturi began to reconstruct his swing. From an onlooker's point of view it appeared that he strengthened his left wrist by shifting the left hand more to the left in the grip, whilst right-hand fingers were more prominent on the shaft. This eliminated any tendency of the left wrist to collapse at impact. Another noticeable feature came after impact when the back of his left hand was kept longer facing the line of flight, thereby keeping the clubface open and inducing a fade. Gradually confidence and the old flair returned. Gone was the unwanted hook. The magic touch on the greens worked like a charm. Climax came with sensational victory in the 1964 U.S. Open, plus two further tournament wins; 1965 saw a temporary set-back with a recurrence of circulatory trouble in his hands, but he still produced consistent golf in the Ryder Cup match. Venturi has proved that a swing can be remodelled and rebuilt with remarkable results, and that in that reconstruction the hands are the focal point.

42. Queen of the Fairways

The golf writer has no illusions about the headline heroes he creates. Rarely does he believe in them, probably because he knows them so well. Occasionally an exception occurs. I think of one golfer for whom I have tremendous respect. I dislike superlatives, yet this is one of the rare occasions when they can be used. I would name Lady Heathcoat-Amory as one of the greatest golfers ever to strike a ball. In the days when she was Joyce Wethered, her style was the perfect demonstration of how a golf ball should be struck. None came within sight of the peak she reached in her prime. There was an incisive crispness about her iron play that is seldom seen in women's golf. Moreover, although she could hold her own against any male player —she proved that against Bobby Jones in a four-ball practice match at St. Andrews— there was no over-masculinity about her game. Unfortunately her days of competitive golf have passed. Those of this generation know her only by name and repute. To their mental picture I add these touches. Joyce Wethered embodied the skill of Harry Vardon, the consistency of Bobby Jones, and the concentration of Henry Cotton in a frame that personified feminine grace, charm and modesty.

This style study shows how she played a shot of her nomination. Her iron shots ruled the pin and were played with the knife-like sharpness usually associated with a professional. In this sequence it is instructive to note the open stance, which in itself shortens the backswing and gives greater control. The photograph after impact is interesting. The swing has reached the point where the power produced by the body has been supplemented by increased infusion from arms, hands and right side. The left side has tensed up to withstand the powerful onslaught. One idiosyncrasy persists—as it did throughout this distinguished player's career—both heels are off the ground at impact. The mannerism is contrary to orthodox teaching which maintains that the left heel should be on the ground at impact, but it has become an established feature of several top-ranking players, such as those shown on pages 98–99. It must therefore be accepted as an unconscious counter to the pull of the swing.

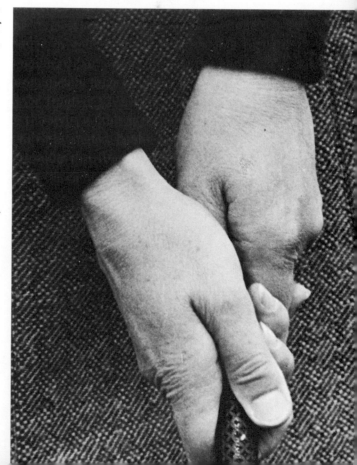

Comparisons are dangerous and often misleading, but I feel safe from contradiction when I say that Lady Heathcoat-Amory hit the ball straighter than any other woman. She lacked the power of "Babe" Zaharias, who could belt the ball out of sight, but what was lacking in strength was more than made up by elegance and style. Her iron shots were flawless. No one could fault her wood shots, whilst her short game, on and around the greens, was brilliant. Moreover, she was equally good at match- or medal-play. The secret lay in her hands. Her grip inspired confidence. It was firm, without a hint of poker-like tension. Placement repays study. You see here one of the most famous grips the game has known.

43. *Hitting Through*

These words must be taken literally. The club must hit *through* the ball. It has long been a truism that a sound follow-through is the postscript to a good swing and not the cause of it. This maxim has led to the belief that the speed of the club is sufficient to carry the body into the correct position, that that is all there is to it, and that physical relaxation after impact automatically produces the desired effect. The fallacy of such a lazy theory is exposed on any course during a week-end. These are the points to note. There is no braking at impact. The grip has stayed firm, even though the ball is far down the fairway. In each case the player has hit through the ball. The hands are going out after the ball. The left hip has moved out of the way of the hands. The right side has infused power into the shot against the tension of the left side. The position of the head is interesting. It is firmly anchored. The players have hit past their chin, which still points to the place where the ball has been.

(*b*) *Sebastian Miguel* (*Spain*)   (*c*) *Jimmy Thomson* (*USA*)

(*d*) *Jack Knipe* (*England*)   (*e*) *Bobby Halsall* (*England*)

(*a*) *Claude Harmon* (*USA*)

a

Alex Kyle (Scotland)

François Saubaber (France)

44. Head Down

"Keep your eye on the ball" is the most overworked maxim in golf. The catch-phrase has become a fetish. It is necessary to distinguish between *looking up* and *rising up*. The latter causes the topped shot. The temptation is always great to look towards the hole before the ball is played. The average player wants to see the entire flight. To do so he often tries to play the shot from memory. The eyes never consciously look at the ball. Deliberate attempts to keep the head down often aggravate the trouble. A compromise is indicated. Many well-known golfers *look up* to see what has happened to a shot. If you must look, you can do the same provided the move is made in only one direction, i.e. laterally from side to side. If you raise your head upwards, the shoulders will rise, the back will straighten, the hands draw in, and the shot will be topped. *Your eye must be kept on the ball right up to the moment of impact.* After that—and I repeat, if you must, and provided you do not rise up—it will be safe for you to look round. Advocates of this tip will assure you that the movement helps to remove any tendency to brake the follow-through and lessens the risk of having the right shoulder blocked off. Even so, I prefer to see the head set about three inches behind the ball at impact, and kept in that position until the arms flow out and the ball is speeding down the fairway. I can do no better than commend to your scrutiny the examples set by these distinguished action studies.

Henry Cotton (England)

Lloyd Mangrum (USA)

124

(a) Fred Haas (USA)

45. *Arm Extension in Follow-through*

This is a continuation of the process of *hitting through* the ball. In each of these examples the clubhead is flowing out along the line of flight; they show quite clearly how the arms, hands and club should go together. There is no suggestion of hurried hitting. The elbows are close together. There is no hint of the left arm collapsing. The angle of the shoulders indicates that the body has stayed behind the shots. All three have hit past the chin and the head is down in approved fashion. The grip is still firm. This feature is easy to test in your own case. At the completion of a shot, the grip ought to be firm enough to address a ball without regripping. The left foot often swivels slightly towards the line of flight. The left side is braced. The right side comes through smoothly. Note the position of right heel, left elbow and right shoulder. Remember that when the clubhead follows out after the ball, the shot has been from the inside. An interesting comparison is to study swings at the top of the backswing and at the completion of the shot. This will show that the follow-through in its completed form is the same as the top of the backswing in reverse, but only if the flowing extension of the arms is the same as these shots by Haas (*a*), King (*b*) and Collins (*c*).

(b) Sam King (England)   *(c) Bill Collins (USA)*

46. Lateral Shift for Hands and Arms

These three action studies are object-lessons to those who hit too soon, a tendency that upsets weight transference. The bent right side indicates the power that has been generated. The head is still anchored. The lateral shift is taking the hips round in smooth fashion; the natural flowing action of the shot will bring the body face on to the line of flight. The balance is perfect. It looks an automatic postscript to a shot, but it is not as simple as all that. Too many golfers swing their shoulders round after impact, but leave their hips fixed, eliminating any suggestion of a lateral shift; or else swipe the ball with the weight piled on the right foot. The result is a spoilt shot. One of the dangers of analysing the mechanism of a shot is that the fact that the swing is a rhythmic whole becomes obscured. From the point of view of instruction it is necessary to refer to the roles played by the legs, hips, arms, body, hands and so on, but in the shot itself the club is not swung by the arms alone. The swing is a fluent co-ordination of the whole.

(*Opposite*) *Frank Stranahan* (*USA*)

D. Hayes (*South Africa*)   *Alberto Salas* (*Chile*)

47. Pronation

Any keen student of the game could not look for better material than analysing the style of Henry Cotton (*a*). He is about the only professional in Britain to have subjected his own style to meticulous examination. He not only knows what he does, but why he does it. Cotton's style is stripped of inessential trimmings. It has brought him three Open Championships and three P.G.A. Match-play titles, and repays careful study. The feature that I want to pin-point in this action study is the way his right hand has climbed over the left. Pronation in the full sense of the word means turning over the right hand as the club approaches impact. The idea is that it produces overspin, which is particularly useful in a long run-up shot. On the other hand, the stroke calls for split-second accuracy in execution. Too much or too little can only result in an indifferent shot. In the full shot the very momentum of the stroke can sweep the hands forward and over in a natural flowing action. The two other examples recall memories of Americans who made many friends in this country. Dick Chapman (*b*) is one of the few top golfers who look upon the golfing scene as a sport, almost an "amateur" sport, whilst Billy Joe Patton (*c*) is an amiable figure, utterly informal and unpretentious. There is no panache, no affectation. He looks like a forgetful college lad, and plays golf in swashbuckling fashion.

(*Opposite*) *Henry Cotton* (*England*)

(*b*) *Dick Chapman* (*USA*)   (*c*) *Billy Joe Patton* (*USA*)

48. Canadians in Action

(I) STAN LEONARD

Stan Leonard is not an easy man to get to know. He can be difficult, obstinate and tough, but once the brusque Canadian surface is penetrated a warmer, convivial individual is revealed. It is the same with his shot-making ability. We in Britain have not seen the brilliance that has earned him such a fine reputation across the Atlantic. This series of action shots was taken during the Canada Cup match in 1963 at the Golf de Saint-Nom-la-Bretèche near Paris. All four are copybook examples of what should be copied. Take the address position. The keynote of the grip is firmness. It has to be in iron shots—if anything, firmer than with wood. Playing a shot off a tee leaves a greater margin of safety even if the grip is slightly relaxed. Play an iron shot with the same grip and the jar at impact when the clubhead bites into the turf will twist the club in the hands. The grip must be firm enough to resist such a twist. The wrists are also firmer than with woods. The balance in the downswing study is good. The pull of the left arm is bringing the right elbow nearer to the body. Note the angle of the right hand. A fault to be avoided is the tendency to bend the left wrist outwards at the top of the backswing. The movement "shuts" the clubface and invites a sharp hook. The shot has come to its completion in the final two studies. The swing has brought the iron through in natural fashion. The grip is still firm.

(II) AL BALDING

Another Canadian who has yet to produce his best form in British events is Al Balding. He is as affable as Leonard is taciturn. He has a single-minded persistence and is almost exasperating in his thoroughness. He has that rare quality of making everything look easy and effortless—the hall-mark of a really great player.

The backswing studies are interesting in that they focus attention on the controversial question of a straight left arm. High-speed photography has proved this to be possible. The left arm can be kept straight to the top of the backswing. The value of this is that it widens the arc of the backswing. The clubhead flows through a line that gives it more time to make the impact squarely. On the other hand, with quite a number of players such a position is physically impossible. They were never intended by Nature to be so supple. The obvious remedy is not to try the impossible. Every golfer has the answer himself. The last three fingers of the left hand determine the issue. Immediately the grip weakens, that is as far as you can go. It is no use having a poker-straight left arm if it ruins your grip. If you can be like Balding, so much the better. If not, allow for individual modification, so long as the arm is straight at impact.

It is always a pleasure to watch Balding in action. His swing is so smooth and deliberate that a mistake seems out of the question. It is possible to feel the rhythm of the movements, which is more than you can say about the average golfer. So many shots are ruined through snatched backswings. Although it is dangerous to dogmatize on speeds of backswings, as it is essentially a point that each individual has to decide for himself, nevertheless one thing is certain. If the backswing is rushed, accurate timing is destroyed, for you are unable to gauge and control the role of

the hands and the clubhead during the shot.

Still on the question of the straight left arm, it is instructive to study Balding at the address and first stage of the backswing. In both examples it would be impossible to fault him on any point. The head is well over the ball, which is addressed in one instance practically in line with the right heel. The ball shifts farther back through the range of irons. With long irons the ball is played off the left heel.

49. Golf in Adversity

Anyone who watches Group-Captain Bader, who lost both legs during the war, playing golf, maybe in a meeting of the Royal Air Force Golfing Association at Moor Park, or the Bowmaker Foursomes, senses the tremendous encouragement he must give to others similarly disabled by war or accident. Certain team games, like cricket, hockey, rugby or Association football are usually out of the question for those not sound in body, limb or vision, although there are always exceptions, men and women who refuse to accept the inevitable. Blindness is generally regarded as the greatest handicap in the participation of any ball game. Golf is one of the games open to those unable to see. I watched Charles Tooth, president of the Canadian Blind Golfers' Association, prove this when, partnered by George Duncan, he returned a round of 66 over 9 holes at Mere Country Club. The professional explained each hole to him, and set his stance. Tooth's average drive was 150 yards. On the green he felt the turf and paced the distance. He sank one putt of 10 yards. I was interested to hear him describe how the affliction had made his hands doubly sensitive. He played by "feel". There was no question of checking backswing, pivot, follow-through. All he could do was "feel" the shot. Once he had the right grip and felt his hands were right, he played the stroke. From the appearance viewpoint, his stroke-play was most convincing.

I can think of other instances. Dr. W. H. Oxenham, blinded in the First World War, never having seen a golf course, bought a set of clubs, learnt by "feel", and became good enough to take part in exhibition matches in America. Gerald Lowry had his optic nerve shattered by a bullet, but became so adept at golf that his drives ranged from 150 to 250 yards. Tommy Armour, former Open champion, had the vision of one eye affected in the First World War, but his record did not suffer. The main pleasure that blind golfers receive in playing the game is the joy of *hearing* and *feeling* a successful shot.

With the amputation of a leg, increased emphasis is placed on arms and hands. C. Sellick lost a leg in a pit disaster, but refused to let the accident interfere with his golf. He became Notts Champion and reached the last sixteen in the English Championship. Ernest Jones had his right leg smashed by shrapnel, but became one of America's finest teaching professionals. Perhaps most remarkable of all was the case of Thomas McAuliffe. He lost both arms as a result of a childhood accident. Necessity forced him to use his teeth to such an extent that his proficiency attracted vaudeville offers. Instead he turned to golf. Holding the clubs between his right shoulder and cheek, he could drive 150 yards and over. Eventually golf became his livelihood and there were few courses over which he could not break 100.

(Opposite) Douglas Bader

50. *Irish Hands*

(I) JOE CARR

Critics used to say that Joe Carr was too easy-going, too gay, too reckless, too nice and too self-indulgent to make a success of championship golf. They had to eat their words. I admit the Irishman has about him an air of gambling optimism, but beneath the veneer is a brilliant, if unconventional golfer capable of beating all comers. With him it is essential that the onlooker discriminate between individualistic mannerisms and basic fundamentals. Analyse the action study on the opposite page. The camera has frozen the swing at a vital stage of a shot. It is just here that so many golfers tie themselves into an unnatural position, with balance upset and taut muscles destroying the rhythmic movement of the swing. Carr demonstrates a copy-book swing. The shoulders are moving round. The right elbow is coming in to the body. Note the pulling action of left shoulder and arm. Power generated by the body is about to be reinforced by the action of hands and arms. On the other hand, pin-pointing the exact stage of the swing when clubhead acceleration becomes stepped-up is almost impossible. So many factors have to be considered. Golfers with strongly developed arms and wrists often hit late and delay acceleration. Such a model would be disastrous for the weaker player who must gauge the physical and psychological moment to release driving-power. Carr's recovery shot can be copied by every class of player. Arms away from body. Note right hand and position of forefinger. The American, Doug Sanders, watched the ball finish by the pin.

(II) HARRY BRADSHAW

There is no one quite like Harry Bradshaw, which is more the pity. Everyone closely connected with professional golf has a feeling of affection for this comfortably built Irishman with a sailor's rolling gait. Affable, genial, he ambles round the course with a generally unbuttoned look, but appearances are deceptive. Behind the rustic Irish exterior is an incisive, technical shot-maker. Admittedly he has certain idiosyncrasies about his swing. It is easy to pick him out in the distance by finger-prints of style. On the other hand, his game is based on sound principles. Archie Compston's advice was based on common sense when he said, "The correct order of the downswing is left hip, left shoulder, left hand, and then the clubhead." Harry Bradshaw is walking confirmation of that adage.

Ben Hogan (USA)

Lloyd Mangrum (USA)

51. Follow-through Determines Head Movement

There should be no restriction to the follow-through. Impact appears the most important part of the swing. Actually it is purely incidental. The swing is only complete when the player hits through the ball. Conscious attempts to check the club immediately after impact are indicative of a jerky swing. The follow-through can indicate what has happened to the shot. The player whose shoulders have come round but whose hips remain static usually has the weight still on the right foot. Result—a slice. If the right shoulder finished above the left, it usually means that it led the clubface in the downswing. The clubface cuts across the ball at impact. Result—a slice. Another indication of the weight still being on the right foot is when the player sways backward after impact, due also to hitting too soon. An artificial follow-through is often seen where the player pulls his arms upward instead of allowing the club to flow out after the ball. Another common failing is when the complete absence of pivot renders impossible any natural form of follow-through. If you cannot get through your shots, the odds are that you are not staying behind the ball with your right shoulder. The best cure is to check the weight-shift from the right foot for a shade longer. The result should be along the lines of these three style studies. There is no suggestion of the head being held back in a clamp-like vice. The natural action of the arms and club has brought the head round in smooth fashion. Hogan's typical finish (*far left*) has the hall-mark of balance and poise.

Mrs. John Beck (Ireland)

52. Youth and Age

The reasons why many long-handicap golfers never improve their game would make a long list. High up would rank the habit of slavishly imitating some well-known golfer. At times the practice can be harmful. Analyse the styles of the world's leading players in this book. Two facts emerge. All observe certain fundamental principles that determine the golf swing, but alongside comes an extensive variation in style. Form and style must not be taken as one and the same thing. Style is the harvest from good form. It is dependent upon the physical and mental make-up of the individual. It is possible that the individual traits of the golfer you seek to copy are alien to your own temperament. Remember that sound style is acquired through learning sound form but it is not always possible to acquire sound form by imitating style. The finger-prints of golf style are rarely duplicated in every detail. Many golfers who begin the game in middle life experience difficulty in getting the body to obey readily during the swing. Analyse the game of a player who just manages to break the hundred-mark. Very often part of the trouble is due to the solidity of the left hip. Unless the left hip can swivel freely, the swing is out of joint. If it is locked, practise a series of swivel actions until the movements are smooth and rhythmic. On the other hand, only the body suppleness of youth could reproduce the flamboyant finish of Marguerita Giden (*left*). Age and maturity must be content with a more abbreviated postscript to a shot.

(*Opposite*)
Marguerita Giden (*Sweden*)

(*Right*) *Ted Ray* (*England*)

(a) Arnold Palmer in a typical finish

53. *Firm Postscript to a Shot*

The follow-through is an essential part of a shot. Far too many imagine that all is over once the moment of impact is reached. On the contrary the follow-through is an accurate indicator of what went before. Allowance must be made for the fact that there are many different types. There is no hard-and-fast rule about finishing. Every player has distinctive finger-prints of style. Much depends on how a player uses wrists and shoulders. If you examine these photographs, every man has used his hands and arms to strike the ball. Even though they are different, each one has the hall-mark of rhythmic timing. Some complete a shot with hands high and right side well through. A player with a flat finish would have hands level with the left shoulder. Reginald Whitcombe used to abbreviate his finish so much that the left hand was almost touching the left shoulder. Gary Player is distinctive at the end of a full-blooded drive. He sweeps through and round with the hips square to the line of flight. The natural flowing action of the shot brings the body round in fluent fashion. Arnold Palmer (*a*) has his hands high, likewise Jean Garaialde (*d*) and Jack Nicklaus (*k*). Max Faulkner (*f*) has a follow-through in its fullest sense. In every case, the grip is firm, particularly the left hand. It is no idle statement to say that no two golfers swing alike.

(*b*) *Eric Brown has a decided body-sway*

(*c*) *Gary Player's natural flowing action*   (*d*) *Jean Garaialde, a firm but fluent finish*

(e) *Hsieh Yung-Yo, excellent balance and poise*

(f) *Max Faulkner, no brake applied here*

(g) *Dick Meyer, smooth postscript to a powerful drive*

(h) *Jimmy Adams, shortened grip but firm finish*

(i) *Jack Burke has hands high and elbows spread*

(j) *Ernest Millward has a knife-like finish*

(k) *Jack Nicklaus's follow-through speaks for itself*

54. Four-stage Summary

(I) The golf grip is basically a problem of pressures. The last three fingers of the left hand determine whether the shot will be accurate or otherwise. The action study of Sam Snead (*below, centre*) epitomizes the copybook position at this stage of the shot.

Jorgen Korfitzen (Denmark)

Sam Snead (USA)

Henning Kristensen (Denmark)

(II) The camera freezes the swing of three champions at a vital stage of a shot. The early stage of the downswing is under left-hand guidance. It is essential to become left hand conscious.

Gary Player (South Africa)　　　*Tony Lema (USA)*　　　*Bob Charles (New Zealand)*

150

(Left) Hsieh Yung-Yo (China)

(Below left) Neil Coles (England)

(Below) Len Nettlefold (Tasmania)

(III) The clubhead speed has been accelerated through the uncocking of the wrists. The right forearm injects force into the drive as the wrists lash the clubhead into the ball. Correct hand placement ensures that the clubface is square at impact.

(IV) The follow-through is an accurate indicator of what went before. The flowing action of arms and club has brought the body round in fluent fashion. The grip is still firm, particularly the left hand.

Angel Miguel (Spain)   *Roberto de Vicenzo (Argentine)*   *Chen Ching-Po (China)*

55. *The Most Powerful Woman Golfer of all Time*

Mildred "Babe" Zaharias was the most remarkable sporting female America has produced. Her record was unique. She covered the 80-metres Olympic hurdles in 11.3 seconds, hurled a javelin 143 feet 4 inches, tossed a baseball 296 feet, high-jumped 5 feet 5¾ inches, and threw the shot 39 feet ¾ inch. As "Babe" Didrikson she was acclaimed as America's star girl athlete. That was roughly thirty years ago. But fame in athletics is ephemeral. Her name slipped from the headlines. Only memories and record-books remained. When that happened, Mildred Zaharias, wife of a famous wrestler, turned her hand to golf.

I saw her first in the British Ladies' Championship at Gullane in 1947. It was like watching Jack Nicklaus in the Boys' Championship. Her opponents were outdriven fully 100 yards by shots that had the power and snap of a professional. One instance will suffice. On the 540-yard 15th in her match against Frances Stephens, the American only needed a No. 4 iron for her second shot, which she pitched to the back of the green. Steel-like wrists enabled her to lash the clubhead through like Arnold Palmer. Wrist-work is of vital importance in the swing. Here is the source of potential weakness in an average woman golfer's game. The wrists act as hinges. If the player is feminine with no Amazonian pretensions, she can still keep up with lustier opponents by concentrating on perfect timing and smooth wrist-work. So many golf instructors talk airily of cocking the wrists. Of course they must be cocked, but equally important they must be cocked at the right moment. Try to hit a ball with stiff wrists and see what happens. The body takes command of the swing with dire results. Your chances of developing a sound swing with locked wrists are slight.

After the Gullane success Mildred Zaharias turned professional and began a barn-storming tour of the States. In the process she accumulated a bevy of feminine talent, women golfers who had made their names as amateurs and decided that dollars were more useful than silver plate. She visited England with the circus known as Fred Corcoran's young ladies. The golf she produced would have beaten half the field in an Open Championship. Unfortunately her entry for the British Open was refused. It was a pity for she would have upset not a little masculine pride. Tragically she became a cancer victim and died in 1956 at the early age of forty-two. Mildred Zaharias was the giant of women's golf. In that sense, it is foolish to suggest that a long-handicap golfer with weak wrists can model her game on such a woman. The example helps if they will remember that a pretty-pretty swing may look nice, but it does not get you far. The trouble is that they will not hit the ball hard enough. You must wind-up to the fullest extent, and infuse that combined power into the clubhead speed. Intelligent practice will indicate what is your maximum clubhead speed.

Alfred Perry (England)

Bill Branch (England)

56. The Secret of Crisp Iron Shots

Iron shots pay dividends on pin-point accuracy. Woods provide the power shots with preoccupation on distance. Irons are concerned with finding much smaller targets. Long-handicap players find them difficult to master. The most awkward is perhaps No. 2. In the hands of players like Nicklaus, Alliss or any leading professional, the shot becomes a joy to watch. The knife-like crispness is too good to be true. The fault lies with the average golfer who tries to register maximum distance by brute force. The potential flight of a No. 2 shot is 200 yards, but that distance will never be obtained by strength alone. The secret is not far to seek. It is there if you only look for it. Certain basic principles are common. These can be copied deliberately. Take the grip. It is firm without being tense. That is one of the main differences between first-class and indifferent shot-making. On the other hand, a loose grip means a foozled shot; the blade impact with the ground will twist the club in the hands. First necessity then is to adopt a grip that is firm without the sensation that your fingers are cracking.

The stance comes next. Usually it is square with the feet fairly close together. Address the ball opposite the left heel. As the range shortens so the ball is addressed

François Saubaber (France)   *Gerard de Wit (Holland)*

farther back until the short approaches are off the right foot. Notice how there is no overswinging, nor is the pivot exaggerated. If you examine the photographs you will see that the left heel is hardly raised. Saubaber is the exception, but that is one of the Frenchman's idiosyncrasies. The left knee is bent downwards and inwards. I would draw your attention to the study of Alfred Perry (*p. 154*), the British Open Champion of 1935, whose slashing style was not everybody's cup of tea, but what it lacked in finesse was more than compensated by its fighting quality. His iron shots were magnificent. If you study that left arm and grip you will find little to fault. The same can be said of Bill Branch. Never over-robust, he nevertheless more than held his own with more powerful rivals. This pivot question must be emphasized. It is not just a casual back-flip. It occupies a vital role in the swing. If you are overswinging, it means that your wrists have lost control. The right hand is playing too strong a part. The solution is obvious, too obvious, because so many golfers are reluctant to adopt it. Study the sequence of iron backswings and abbreviate yours accordingly.

Carl Poulsen (Denmark)

(Opposite) Bernard Hunt (England)

Remember the basic difference between playing wood and iron shots. It is no use trying to swing both clubs in the same way, yet many golfers do so, forgetting that woods have a sweeping swing with a far greater arc than the abbreviated backswing needed in an iron shot. Another elementary point sometimes overlooked is the simple thing of soling the club properly. If you watch week-end golfers in action, you see many addressing the ball and playing the shot with the iron resting on its heel. The best way is to sole the iron flat on the turf behind the ball then adjust grip and stance. If you turn to the impact photographs, there lies the secret of successful iron play. *The ball, not turf, is taken first by the clubhead*. The downward blow squeezes the ball off the ground. Impact comes before the club touches the lowest arc of the swing. Add to this the finely judged question of weight distribution. Unless it has been shifted to the left side at impact, the club will strike under the ball rather than through it. That is the reason why so many iron shots are mediocre, the insistence on taking a divot behind the ball rather than in front. When the downswing begins, if the weight is still

Max Faulkner (England)   *Ken Bousfield (England)*

Johnny Palmer (USA)

Ed Oliver (USA)

on the right foot, it will stay there throughout the shot. The right side becomes
anchored. It is better to transfer the
weight a shade earlier to the left side
because that will ensure a downward hit
on the ball.

Medium irons have a narrower stance
than the stronger irons. This brings me to
the question of back-spin, a source of envy
to all long-handicap players. Occasionally
they get the ball to pull up by accident,
but few are capable of obtaining the effect
to order. They imagine that if the ball is
sent high enough on its flight to the green,
back-spin is bound to follow. Unfortunately an ascending shot usually has overspin, not back-spin, caused through impact

Robert Sweeny (USA)

Walter Burkemo (USA)   *Peter Alliss (England)*

taking place on the upward arc, both ball and ground being struck at the same time. To get back-spin, the ball must be struck before the turf. Sometimes there is difficulty in getting the ball to rise. It is struck hard enough, but instead of soaring it scuttles along the fairway. The reason is that the ball has been hit too hard—hit, that is, by the right hand with the left hand overpowered. The fault can be checked by looking at the left wrist at the top of the backswing. It should be underneath the shaft, but make sure that the wrist is not bent outwards, a fault that shuts the clubface and causes hooking.

(*Opposite*) *Gene Sarazen* (*USA*)

(*Right*) *Walter Burkemo* (*USA*)

(*Opposite*) *Fred Haas* (*USA*)

Richard Yost (*USA*)

A golden rule of medium-range iron shots is never to under-club. It is so pointless. Why force the club to get those extra yards, when the correct club is in the bag? Far safer to slow down the backswing. Hurrying will only induce jerkiness. Take the club back slowly and begin the downswing on the same note. The result will be a shot under control. Study the effortless appearance of the backswing.

Impact. The hands are just in front of the ball. The arms are not checked at impact. They flow out and through—along the line of flight. The completed shot looks the essence of simplicity. I admit it is deceptive. Professionals do make everything look child's-play. On the other hand, these shots can be mastered by golfers of every age. Sometimes there is the problem of knowing what strength of club to use. On this point, distance-potential is an individual matter. To find out for yourself, practise playing shots forty yards from the green; gradually extend the range and see which club is needed to find the target.

57. Sam Snead Sequence

Sam Snead is still a perpetual phenomenon. He has been playing top-flight golf for so long that his name is now almost a legend, so much so that one tends to associate it only with the past. No greater mistake could be made. In spite of the years, Snead can be as formidable as ever. In the 1965 Open at Birkdale his swing was still the most majestic on view. Every golfing honour has been his, except the one title he would perhaps like most—the U.S. Open. Time and again bad luck barred the way. Now it will probably never be his, but recognition needs no prompting. Either Snead is a genius or the word has no meaning. Even on an off day he is worth a hundred of the neat little *petit-maîtres* of the golfing world.

If a golfer blessed with youth, powerful back and leg muscles, plus a pair of sturdy hands, is looking for a model on which to base his game, he need look no further than this Virginian professional. Here is power golf at its best. In these two photographs taken in 1965, Snead personifies the maxim that the key to a sound swing is a good grip. The placement of hands on the shaft is sensitive yet firm. Studying the hand position of club golfers, it is obvious that lack of control at the top of the swing is frequently due to a weak grip. There is no sign of a "piccolo" grip in the Snead shots, no danger of the left-hand fingers relaxing. It is true that he has exceptionally strong hands, but hands and arms can be strengthened. Several professionals have developed their muscles by swinging a 22-ounce driver. The average driver weighs about 14 ounces. The difference in weight gives rhythmic hand action.

The action sequence on the opposite page of a short iron shot shows no attempt to snatch up the club at the beginning of the backswing. The shot is primarily a downward blow. No hint of reaching for the ball. If that happens the stance is too far from the ball. No scooping at impact with jerky hand movements. The loft of the club has picked up the ball. The follow-through is fluent with the right hand climbing over the left.

58. Two-in-one Shots

These shots are not only stroke-savers, they can be match-winners. The full pitch played with a pitching-wedge can be decisive. I remember how Willie Turnesa literally won the Amateur Championship at Carnoustie with a succession of these shots played with a full swing and fluent follow-through. He took turf, but there was no suggestion of quarrying. From 70 yards the ball was as good as dead. It looks easy to play, and when you know how, it is not too bad, but unless back-spin is applied, the shot might just as well be played with a shovel. There lies the secret. The ball must be struck before the club arrives at the lowest point of its arc. That is how you get back-spin. Meticulous striking of the ball sets up spin in flight which becomes the back-spin action when the ball lands on the green. The best way is to watch professionals playing the shot. At impact you will see that the left arm and club form a straight line. There is no suggestion of scooping. After watching, go out and practise. Keep at it for hours until the knack has been mastered. Score-cards will soon show if you have the shot in the bag. Once mastered, the pitching-wedge is a versatile club with plenty of loft and controlled flight. On sun-baked greens it can be a blessing. But it must be tamed. A foozled wedge shot can be as costly as it might be economic. The medium pitch sets even more importance on the straight left arm continuing through the shaft. In the backswing this straight line is still maintained. Keep that line throughout the shot with smooth transference of weight and no suggestion of forcing. If that is done you will tackle with confidence the delicate loft needed to clear the bunker that so often comes between the ball and the green.

The clearest way to emphasize the basic principles of these short-range shots is to let the camera freeze the swing. Ted Kroll, the stocky professional from New Hartford, New York, is adept at rolling two shots into one. These two studies show clearly the pendulum swing. The shot is virtually played with the hands and arms, the clubhead keeping close to the ground.

(*Opposite and right*) *Ted Kroll* (*USA*)

François Saubaber (France)

It must be remembered that the choice of club for chipping is determined by the loft needed to find the green. The ball must then roll up to the hole. Kroll has taken the club back squarely from the ball. Note the hands and wrists.

Four frontal views of the address. I like particularly the position of François Saubaber, a quietly spoken Frenchman with a wide variety of shots. For a time linguistic troubles proved a handicap, but what he called his *vocalluberry* was irresistible. Note how he has roughly a quarter-turn of the body, perhaps not so pronounced with the other three, but nevertheless a useful tip for many players. The weight is on the left foot. If the weight

Jimmy Demaret (USA)

Al Balding (Canada)

Gary Player (South Africa)

Jimmy Demaret (USA)

was piled on the right foot, or was evenly divided, the shot would probably have been half-topped. Remember that the ball must be hit before the club takes turf. The hands must be close to the body, and the ball addressed opposite the right toe. Keep the feet close together. All four positions look compact.

Merely to study the next four photographs is to sense the swinging motion of the action. In the backswing of Snead, Burkemo and Demaret look at the wrists and straight left arm. The right elbow is in to the side. Then compare them with the downswing of Joe Carr. There has virtually been no body turn, just this fluent swinging-through action. In the

Walter Burkemo (USA)

Joe Carr (Ireland)   *Sam Snead (USA)*

174

Bob Hamilton (USA)

downswing the left arm is still firm, the right elbow tucked in, as the shot develops acceleration and power. Impact position tells its own story. Bob Hamilton, the American Ryder Cup player, is a life-loving individual, bubbling over with infectious good humour, an ingrained optimist when it comes to golf, and endowed with indomitable energy. These traits emerge in his game, which is of the exuberant variety. His short-range accuracy is deadly. It has about it the delicacy of touch normally associated with putting. This impact study shows the wrists straight and clubhead level with the hands. He has probably the strongest left hand, wrist and forearm in the game. Body movement was reduced to a minimum. The same applies to that American stylist, Charles Coe, though in his case, as with Middlecoff, the hands are more advanced. In all three instances the shots were copybook.

Charles Coe (USA)   *Cary Middlecoff (USA)*

The next five action studies show the natural sequence of movement from impact to the follow-through. Balding's position is sound, likewise Bruce Crampton and Peter Thomson. Note the straightened right arm. Bernard Hunt's hands are well worth studying. There has been no suggestion of pulling the club around, instead it has gone out towards the hole, at least 8 or 9 inches. The right arm has straightened. Bernard Hunt is a magnificent golfer. All he needs is to remember the fact and he would be in the Player-Palmer-Nicklaus class. Few can equal his skill in the delicate approach shots. Ted Kroll completes the sequence with a typical fluent finish.

Al Balding (Canada)

Bruce Crampton (Australia)

(Opposite) Bernard Hunt (England)

Peter Thomson (*Australia*)

Finally a word about the shot from off the edge of the green. The choice is usually a chip with a No. 5 iron or the putter. In the photograph Phil Rodgers plumped for the chip. When an average golfer tries this shot he often ruins it through a scooping action, maybe with too lofted a club. He should remember these simple points: hands a trifle ahead of the ball; feet close together; hit the ball first and turf afterwards; virtually no wrist-break. On the other hand, if a putter is used, there is one mistake that many players make. In an attempt to hit the ball harder, the putter is turned back in an instinctive attempt to give it loft. Impact sees the ball dart off the line in unpredictable fashion. The answer is to play the putt as if it were on the green. The ball will then have a genuinely smooth running action.

Ted Kroll (*USA*)

Phil Rodgers (USA)

(a) *Tony Lema (USA)*

(b) *Beverly Hanson (USA)*

59. *Hands Down the Shaft*

Short pitch shots call for meticulous accuracy in timing and judgment, plus a sensitive "feel" of the club. Adopt this tip and you will find that you will be able to play these two-in-one shots with the right amount of "touch"—let your grip go down the shaft just as you see in these four action studies. To begin with Lema's (*a*) may be a shade too far down, but Gary Player's (*d*) is just right. The shots will be more controlled.

(*c*) *Frank Stranahan (USA)*   (*d*) *Gary Player (South Africa)*

60. Recovery Shots

Another name for shot-savers. The obvious stroke is the one that is going to get you out in one shot. Take the ball that finishes in thick grass. Too many players plump for distance as well as safety. The best way is to select a well-lofted club—No. 8 or sand-wedge—use an upright swing and play the ball on the downswing. Johnny Bulla (*a*), that likeable giant of an American who has played in several British Open Championships, is shown playing a shot from fairly thick rough. The recovery in this instance was successful. The head was firmly anchored, and the stance narrow. Another example was burly Phil Rodgers (*b* and *c*), who first of all tried out the club in imagination, then played a brilliant shot from light rough. The ball was struck first before the turf. Clubface was kept open. Position of arms and hands should be noted. The head was kept firm in copybook fashion.

(*a*) *Johnny Bulla* (*USA*)

(*b and c*) *Phil Rodgers* (*USA*)

(d) *Tony Lema (USA)*

The first requirement for a recovery shot out of the rough is to choose a club sufficiently lofted for the job. Tony Lema (d) has taken up a stance close to the ball. The feet are fairly close together. The main thing to remember in these salvage shots is not to attempt too much. Players try to get distances that would be ambitious from the fairway. It is tempting to introduce too much right hand into recovery shots, particularly if the ball rests in a patch thick enough to check the clubhead. In such circumstances the stroke becomes a chopping action in which the right hand automatically feels that it should be in command. The instinct is wrong. The left hand must be in control. It plays the shot from opposite the right foot without following through. In Lema's backswing note the right elbow, left-arm angle of wrists and bent knees. In cases where the grass is really long and impedes the progress of the club, an upright swing is used with the clubface turned slightly back in the downswing. The clubface is square to the ball at impact through the wrists rolling immediately before contact. A firm left-hand grip is essential. If the recovery shot is only for short range, a cut shot is best, but if length is essential, the ball should be played a shade more off the right foot with an upright swing. A sweeping shot is unlikely to succeed for the grass will wrap itself round the shaft. In Eric Brown's recovery shot (e) he had his hands right forward. The clubface made contact with the ball before the grass. The head was firm, the right arm straight, weight distribution good. The ball finished close to the hole.

The permutation of possible recovery shots is almost endless. So many require on-the-spot improvisation that defies the ordinary methods of play. For instance, the American Doug Sanders (f and g) played a brilliant recovery shot from Birkdale rough with the weight firmly lodged on the right foot during a full backswing. The hands repay study. The grip is firm, particularly the left hand. Compare an almost identical-angle photograph of the downswing on another occasion. This time the ball found the rough on the edge of the fairway. The left arm is not so straight. Occasionally a water hazard shot has to be faced. Usually the sensible course is to lift out and incur the penalty. On the other hand, if you insist, take off your shoes and socks, wade in, take an open stance, an open clubface, a No. 9 iron, and aim just behind the ball. What happens is a venture of faith. I advise the coward's way out rather than damping your ardour and spoiling the score-card. More frequently recovery shots are needed to clear a tree. This means a quick-rising shot with a well-lofted club. The drill is simple, but execution difficult. Take a stance more behind the ball. Left foot is taken well back. Right foot advanced. The proposed line of flight looks to be the left of the target. Natural loft of club increased by turning blade out. At impact the clubface hits across the ball. This cut shot gives considerable side-spin as well as back-spin. The ball rises exceptionally quickly. The combined spin usually causes the ball to twist to the right on landing. Care must be taken not to scoop the ball with the clubhead.

Finally a word about the ultimate hazard of the links. Many golfers find their swing put out of joint when winds sweep across the fairways. Often inability to cope

e

(e) *Eric Brown (Scotland)*

(f and g) Doug Sanders (USA)

is due to a wrong approach—mental as well as physical—to the problem. Strength alone gets you nowhere. The long hitter has an advantage in calm weather, but length is quicker out of control in windy weather. It depends whether you oppose or use the wind. Fight the wind and you are backing a loser. It is an education to watch Gary Player playing a push shot with a long iron against the wind. He takes a square stance. Weight on left foot throughout. Clubface square to ball. Very little pivot. The ball is struck first and squeezed against the turf. This nipping of the ball between clubface and ground keeps the flight low, the low-trajectory ball bores into the gale. If you want to flatter yourself, take a driver for playing downwind. Tee the ball high, address the ball off the left toe, and play a sweeping stroke that takes the ball on the upstroke. With the additional help of overspin, considerable distances can be obtained.

Brian Huggett (Wales)

61. Sand Recovery Shots

Bunker shots take a toll of long-handicap players. Blasting wildly in sand does little but bury the ball and worsen the blood-pressure. Most of the difficulties are psychological. If you want to watch how recovery shots ought to be played, take up a position by a well-bunkered green during a championship. The 13th green at Hoylake is an obvious choice. In a high wind the green is missed on innumerable occasions, the ball burying itself in one of the encircling bunkers. When that happens to a poor player the odds are that 8 or 9 will go on the card. With professionals it makes little difference. A regulation 3 is frequently registered. The psychological side of bunkers cannot be overlooked. Many a player, faced with a perfectly simple shot, will make a mess of it because a bunker has to be cleared. If this phobia could be overcome the presence of bunkers would be an aid rather than a hindrance. A green surrounded or flanked by sand-traps is a far better target than one left completely open. The flag is pin-pointed. Concentration is sharpened. The same principle applies to every shot. It is much better for the player to aim at a specific target rather than slamming a ball hopefully into space.

Flory van Donck (Belgium)   *Bobby Halsall (England)*

To master the recovery shot from sand it is essential to size up the stroke intelligently, then refuse to try the impossible. So many times I have seen a player step into a sand-trap and try for distances that he would never get from the fairway with a long-range iron. Often when a professional steps into a bunker and takes his stance, you will notice that he wriggles his feet in the sand. That enables him to get a firm footing, but, more important, it tells him about the texture of the sand. That is where so many players go wrong. They imagine that an explosion shot only needs a cascade of sand for the ball to sail out of the bunker, overlooking the fact that hard sand calls for a wedge shot played off the right foot with a shortened grip, whilst fine sand needs the clubhead to enter the sand even farther behind the ball than usual. This is where high-speed photography helps. At impact the clubhead comes into contact with the sand a few inches behind the ball, and that is the spot the player looks at during the shot. The golden rule for playing a bunker shot is that you must hit down and through the ball. There must be no attempt to check the club or scoop the ball. The blade of the club bites through the sand behind the ball, the club following through with an open clubface. If the shot is shanked, the face of the club has been shut. There are two further points to notice, elementary ones but vital. In every case the head is kept down and the left-hand grip is firm throughout. Assuming that all these points have been noted, successful bunker play is still dependent on one thing . . . practice.

(*Above*) *Neil Coles* (*England*)
(*Below*) *John Jacobs* (*England*)

Without intensive practice, no golfer can step into a bunker feeling confident. Until the "feel" of a shot is known, anything can happen. The usual tendency with sand shots is to chop at the ball.

The cut shot is invaluable if you want a recovery to stop on the green. Remember these four points and the stroke is straightforward. Open stance: open clubface—if you find difficulty in doing this shift your grip farther over until the "V's" aim at your chin; address the ball off the left heel; do not ration wrist action. Do not take much sand and play the stroke from outside in. The spin will apply a fierce brake. Occasionally putting out of bunkers is a stroke worth playing, but the decision must be confident, not born of desperation. The way from the ball to the green must not be barred by a ridge or bank that has to be surmounted. If the shot is to be successful, it must be played like an ordinary lengthy putt. Any attempt to nip the ball over any obstacle is pointless. If this type of shot is needed, then choose the correct club. Provided the ball is lying nicely and the distance to the pin does not require a miniature drive, everything is set for a firm, confident putt. Only experience gained from regular practice can help when it comes to the "feel" and strength of stroke required.

The clean-flick recovery is an effective

(*Above*) *Bobby Halsall* (*England*)
(*Below*) *Jimmy Adams* (*Scotland*)

Norman von Nida (Australia)

Syd Scott (England)   *Max Faulkner (England)*   *Jack Burke (USA)*

but difficult shot. It is essentially a finger-stroke. Flat-footed stance. The work is done by wrists and arms. Nothing tense about the grip. Ball struck firm and clean. If the situation is desperate, length essential, and sand of the loose soft variety, it is the shot to play. On the other hand, it can be a chancy shot. It is not easy to gauge for short recovery. I regard it as a specialized stroke for the expert.

If you find that first-time bunker recoveries are the exception rather than the rule, you have failed to remember one of these nine points: Did you keep your head down? Did you hit down and through the sand without check? Did you try to scoop up the ball? Did you retain your balance throughout the shot? Did you gauge correctly the texture of sand and the amount you took? Did mind and muscle co-operate in making the stroke? Did you know beforehand what type of shot you intended to play? Did you begin the backswing in the approved fashion or was it like the action of wielding a chopper? Did you keep a firm grip, particularly with the left hand? Finally, always use your sand-wedge.

Arnold Palmer (USA)

62. The Game within a Game

Once reach the green and we find a game within a game. It does not take long to realize that the finger-prints of putting style are as individual as the person holding the putter. There is no set method. A successful putter can use a weapon 12 inches long or so elongated in shaft.that the end rests against his chest, like Max Faulkner's choice when he won the Open Championship at Portrush. Take a note of the grips, if only for the sake of experiment. You will find cross-handed, reverse, overlap, one-handed, both hands well down the shaft, croquet-style, and so on. The main thing is to find the one that suits you. That can only happen with practice. One feature is common to all sound putters. You will never see a tense grip. That is the quickest way to kill a sensitive touch. Once lose the "feel" of a putt and you might just as well take up hockey. Do not go to the other extreme with a feather grip that lets the shaft turn in the hands at impact. A grip can be firm without being tense. Some players solve their grip problem by pressing the tip of the right-hand thumb into the side of the shaft. It sounds an odd remedy, but it does help to keep the clubface square to

Doug Sanders and Sam Snead (USA)

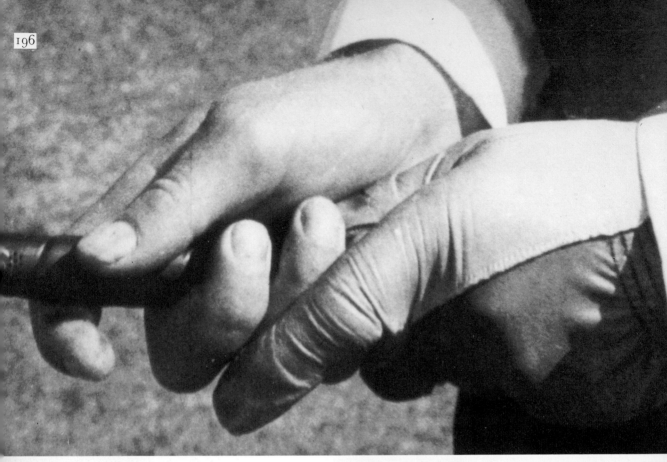

Christy O'Connor (Ireland)

Joe Carr (Ireland)

the line of the putt. Two other points about the grip. When the putt is uphill, tighten it slightly. When putting downhill, loosen the grip a fraction. I am sure that uncertainty about the grip disturbs the rhythm of the putt. On the score of popularity, choice of grip would go to the reverse overlap grip.

Choice of stance is as varied as grips. Once again the best advice is to note what the experts do and try out their methods. Remember that the majority of brilliant putters do not stand a long way from the ball. Control is more difficult if you do. Some players use a close upright stance and right-handed action. Others prefer a wider, open stance with the weight forward and the ball opposite the left heel. Some have a close stance with the left foot behind the right. Others have feet together, weight evenly balanced, and knees slightly stiff to counter body-sway. Some have an upright stance with arms away from the body. One of the most popular stances with professionals is slightly open with the right foot ahead of the left foot. The feet are not very far apart. The weight is on the left foot. A couple of points to remember. To counter a tendency to cut across the ball adopt a closed stance. A tendency to push putts out can be checked if the ball is a shade in front of the centre of the clubface. Also note that stances are usually wider when the wind is strong to ensure a firmer base.

Harry Weetman (England)

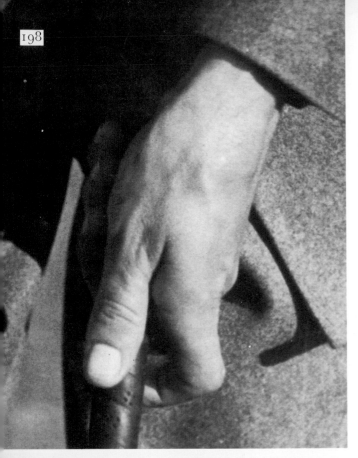

A characteristic common to most first-class players is the act of soling the putter in front of the ball at the address. Various theories have been put forward to account for this mannerism. I have been told it eases tension, acts as a muscle-rehearsal for the putt, helps to line-up the stroke. There are several other views. One thing is certain. For some reason or other soling the putter does help. It becomes part of a reassuring ritual and strengthens confidence. Anything that helps on the green is worth several shots a round. On the other hand, be careful not to move the ball when soling the putter. Another point to

Mario Gonzalez (Brazil)

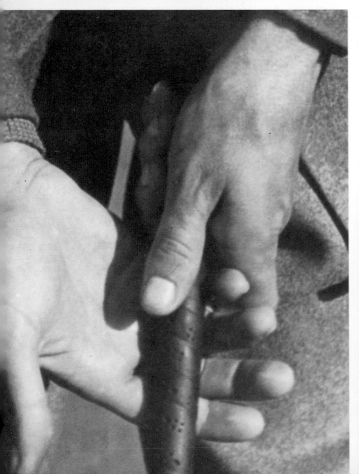

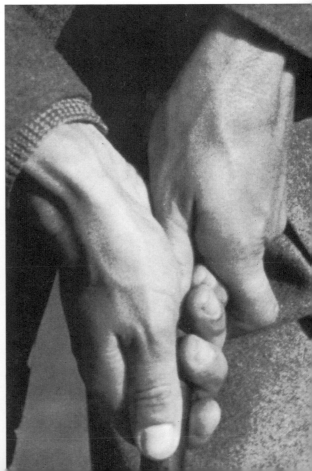

notice when the player is addressing the putt is that the majority would pass the old test of a coin dropped from the bridge of the nose landing on the ball. The eye is directly over the ball. That may not be everybody's choice, but it is the preference of the majority of champions. It is true that the majority of players pin-point the ball with their eyes when they are putting. The fact remains that some golfers discover that they putt better if they pin-point the hole with their eyes as they putt. One warning must always be heeded—head up and a jab invariably results.

Charles Ward (England)

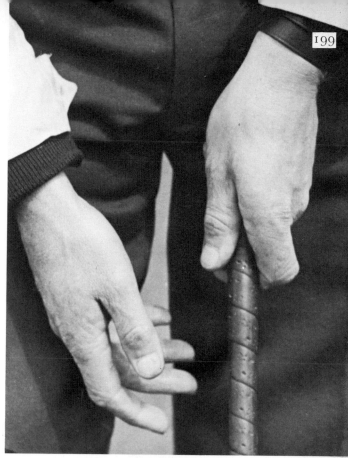

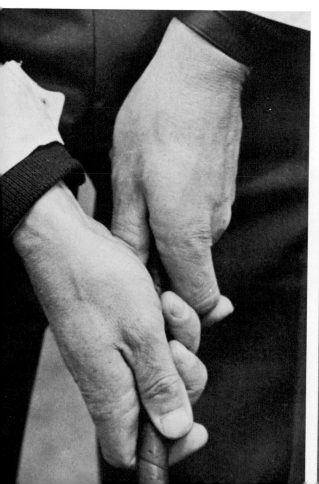

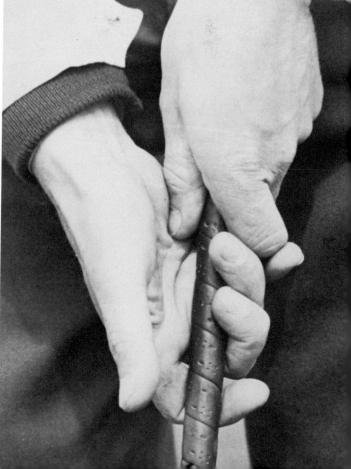

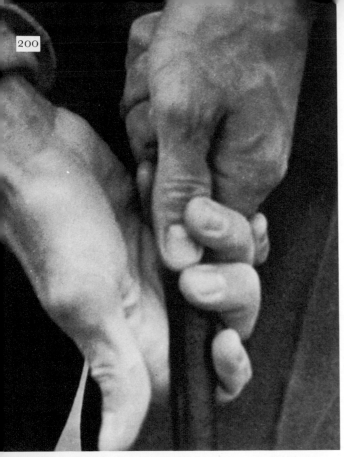

The backswing is almost universal in its orthodox movement. The blade is taken back low and square to the hole with a slow rhythm. At impact the blade is kept at right angles to the line of the putt. There is no suggestion of stabbing. The head is anchored. If you study carefully you will see that all movement of head, shoulders and hips is eliminated. Compare the action with a week-end golfer. Head up and half-topped putts, with the left hand often turned over at impact or the ball struck with the heel of the putter, the action resembling a stab. When the wind is strong, pay particular attention to the

Bill Branch (England)

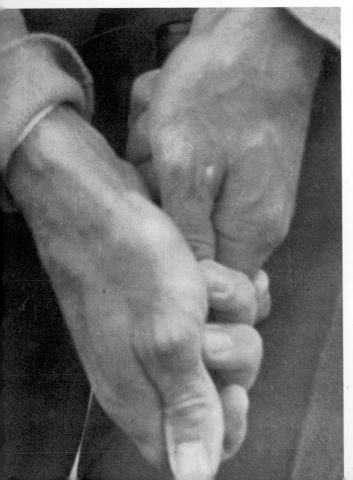

way the "borrow" is anticipated by playing for the windward side of the tin. In a high wind the backswing can be slightly modified. Should the downswing cut across the ball, a check-up will show that the fault is due to taking the clubface back outside the line of the putt. In certain cases the hands are a shade more forward during the backswing. I have also noticed that many professionals use a longer backswing on approach putts. On greens that slope from left to right, give the putt a chance by putting to the left side of the hole. Once again, never stab at the ball.

Stanley Bishop (USA)

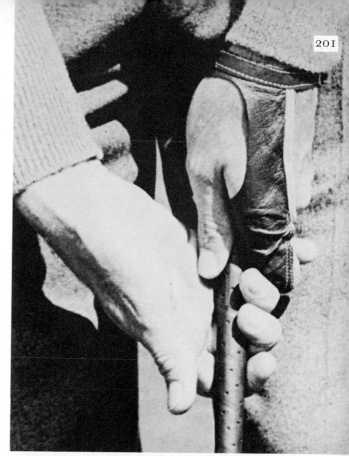

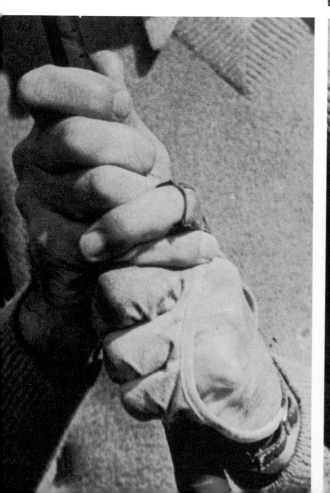

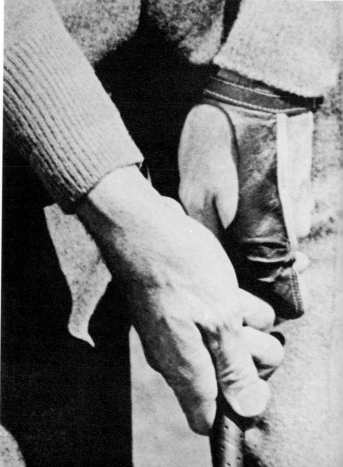

The follow-through must mean something. It must be real. The clubhead should stroke through the ball. The rhythmic, flowing movement along the line of the putt helps to eliminate errors in direction. The blade hugs the ground. The length of the follow-through is about the same as the backswing, though some players argue that a longer follow-through helps direction. It is not a meaningless postscript but the unhurried completion of the stroke. The head must be anchored until the ball is on its way to the hole, though some players move the head side-

Flory van Donck (*Belgium*)

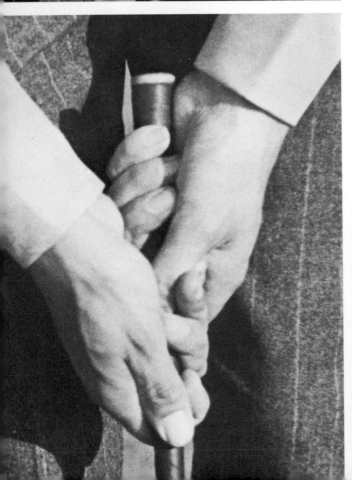

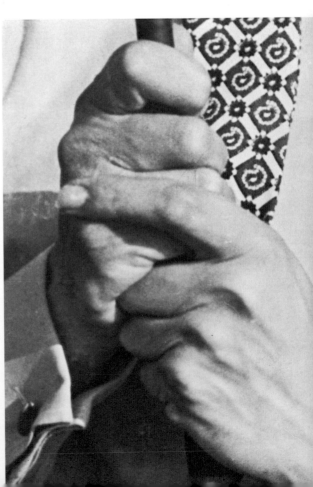

ways to see what is happening, but in relation to the body the position is unaffected. One point receives general approval. Body action is eliminated. If you play a putt without follow-through, you have either relaxed your grip, lifted your head, or struck an over-hurried putt. It will be a stabbing movement, with the ball probably short.

A word about reading the greens. This varies from player to player. Some are quick and decisive, others flop about on the green for what seems like hours. The first thing to remember is that the drill is

Beverly Hanson (USA)

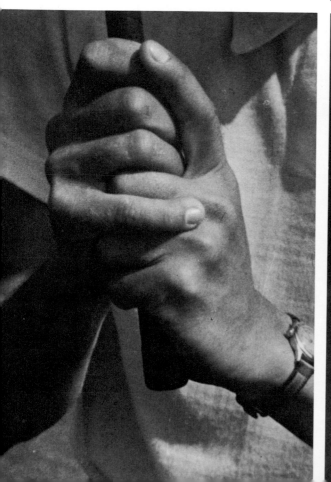

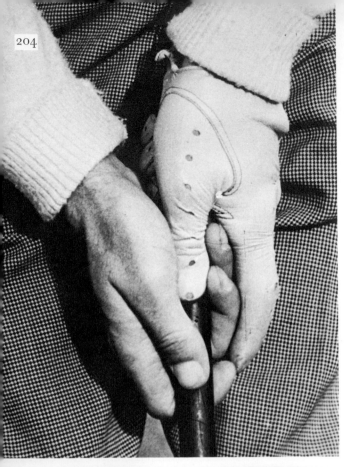

useful. It is the only way to putt intelligently. But you must know what you are doing. Set your own routine and keep to it every time you putt. Contours and slopes must be studied, particularly within a few feet radius of the hole. Examine the line from behind the hole. Do the same from the other side of the hole. Loose impediments on the line should be removed. Check the grain of the grass. Remember these tips. The ball runs farther with the grain: against, the pace will be slower. Grains left to right across the hole means that the putt must be played slightly to the

Eric Brown (Scotland)

(Below left) Eric Brown (Scotland)

Harold Paddock (USA)

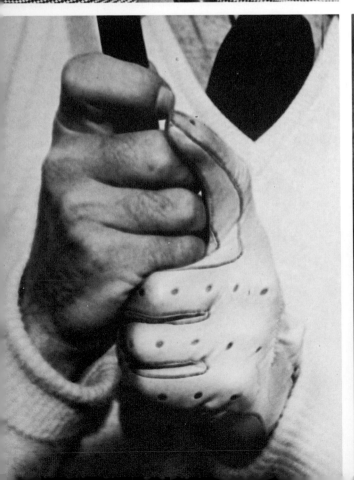

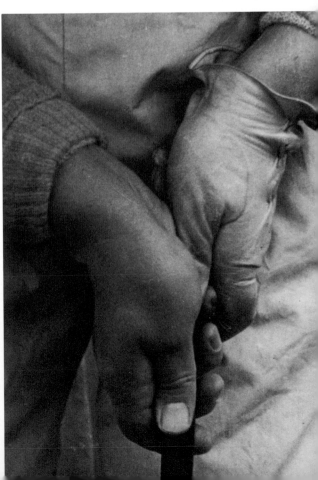

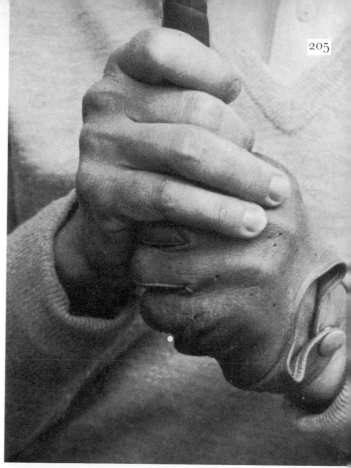

left: grain right to left, putt struck a little to the right. Gauging the pace of the green is important and can only come with practice. Decide the line and strike the ball so that it rolls over a point selected about a yard from the hole. Bear these pointers in mind when you study professionals preparing to putt. Remember that missed putts are usually caused by mis-reading, not mis-hitting. Do not be afraid of getting down behind the ball and studying the line. Ultimately practice is the answer. Practice breeds confidence and putting is seventy-five per cent confidence.

Friedel Becker (Germany)

(Below right) Harry Bradshaw (Ireland)

Antonio Cerda (Argentine)

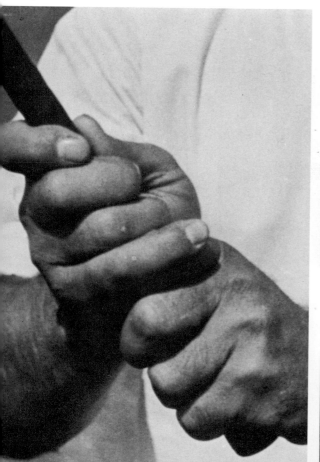

Sonia Eloy (France)

Bill Collins (USA)

(Opposite)
Diana Critchley
(England)

(*Above*) *Ronnie Shade* (*Scotland*)
(*Opposite*) *Bob Charles* (*New Zealand*)

Doug Sanders (USA)   *Flory van Donck (Belgium)*   *Al Balding (Canada)*

Chen Ching-Po (China)   *Christy O'Connor (Ireland)*

Tommy Bolt (USA)

Cary Middlecoff (USA)

Charles Ward (England) *Ben Hogan (USA)* *Jack Burke (USA)*

Jack Nicklaus (USA)

Roberto de Vicenzo (Argentine)

Peter Thomson (Australia)

John Jacobs (England)

Mario Gonzalez (Brazil)

Myong Chul Park (Korea)

(Below left)
Dick Chapman (USA)

(Below right)
Charles Coe (USA)

Jerry Barber (USA)

Douglas Bader

Neil Coles (England)

George Bessner (Germany)

James Braid (Scotland)

"Skip" Alexander (USA)

Joe Carr (Ireland)

(*Opposite*) *Ken Venturi* (*USA*)
(*Right*) *Arne Werkell* (*Sweden*)
(*Below left*) *Enrique Bertolino* (*Argentine*)
(*Below right*) *Helen Lawson-Page* (*USA*)

Jimmy Turnesa (USA)

Harry Bradshaw (Ireland)   *Bill Branch (England)*

(*Above right*) *Tom Haliburton* (*England*)
(*Below left*) *T. D. Dill* (*USA*)
(*Below right*) *Francis Smith* (*England*)

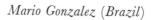
Mario Gonzalez (Brazil)

rnold Palmer (USA)   Cary Middlecoff (USA)

(Above left) Bill Branch (England)
(Above right) Duk Choon Yun (Korea)
(Right) Gary Player (South Africa)
(Opposite) Ben Hogan (USA)

(*Right*) *Peter Thomson (Australia)*
(*Below left*) *Fred Daly (Ireland)*
(*Below right*) *Gene Sarazen (USA)*

(Above left) Friedel Becker *(Germany)*
(Above right) Ugo Grappasonni *(Italy)*
(Left) Luis Rapisarda *(Brazil)*

Lionel Platts (England)

(Opposite) Sam Snead (USA)

Harry Weetman (England)

(*Above left*)
Francis Smith (*England*)

(*Above right*)
James Adams (*Scotland*)

(*Left*)
Max Faulkner (*England*)

(Left)
Lloyd Mangrum (USA)

(Below left)
Enrique Bertolino (Argentine)

(Below right)
Roberto de Vicenzo (Argentine)

(Above left)
Henry Cotton (England)

(Above right)
Gerard de Wit (Holland)

(Left)
Mario Gonzalez (Brazil)

Tony Lema (USA)

(*Opposite*) *Peter Thomson* (*Australia*)
(*Above left*) *Antonio Cerda* (*Mexico*)
(*Above right*) *Stanley Bishop* (*USA*)
(*Right*) *Bill Branch* (*England*)

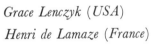

Grace Lenczyk (USA)
Henri de Lamaze (France)

Ben Hogan (USA)

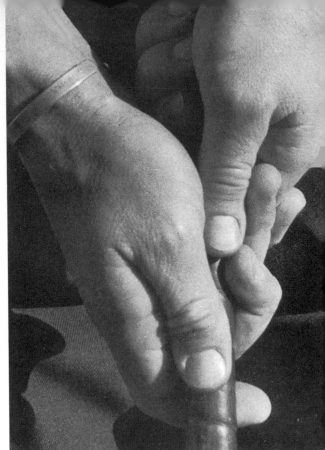

63. Peter Butler on the Green

There is no such thing as a regulation putting style. No other club in the bag attracts so many theories. The main criterion is whether the ball drops into the tin. It is essentially an individual problem. It is safe to say, however, that Peter Butler is the embodiment of orthodox consistency on the green. He has a firm grip with sensitive and controlling fingers. Note in particular the placement of the thumbs on the shaft. There is no hint of tension in the grip, that bugbear that ruins the feel. A delicate putting grip usually follows a sensitive touch. It does so in Butler's case. A light grip with body-sway virtually eliminated and no head movement usually produces the best result. The shot is an action of wrists, hands and arms without any suggestion of stabbing.

64. *Finger-prints of Style to Study*

(I) JIMMY THOMSON (USA)

The way hands are placed on the club determines the degree of control over the shot.
Grip must be firm but not rigid.
The "V" formed by index finger and thumb points over the right shoulder.
Note the use of left-hand glove.

(II) GARY PLAYER (South Africa)

Arms hang naturally from the shoulders. Hands fractionally ahead of the clubhead.
Note placement of thumbs on shaft.

(*Opposite*) *Gary Player* (*South Africa*)

Jimmy Thomson (*USA*)

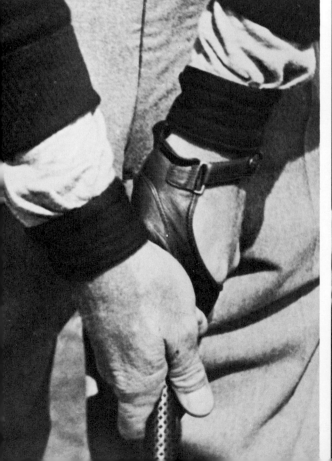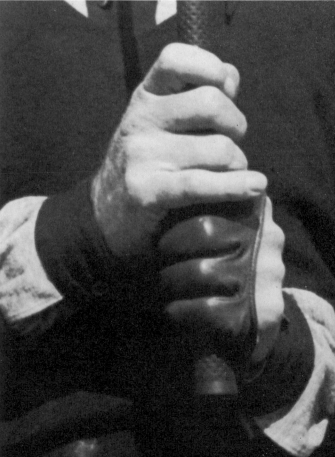

(III) GARY PLAYER (South Africa)

The start of the swing is neither a turn nor a lift. It is a combination of two movements.

The club is pushed back with the hands, wrists and arm.

Left arm straight.

Clubhead close to ground.

(IV) KEN BOUSFIELD (England)

No attempt to snatch the club up.
Left shoulder shifting around under the chin.
Wrist-cock about to begin.
Left hip turning to right.
Weight transferring to right foot.

(V) HENRY COTTON (England)

The pivot is not an artificial movement. It is a natural, rhythmic turn of the body.
Left shoulder points at ball.
Firm grip on shaft.

(VI) LIONEL HERBERT (USA)

The vital part of the swing.
The left hand and left arm have taken the club back.
Wrists cocked. Grip firm.
In this position there is a feeling of both power and control.

(VII) BILL COLLINS (USA)

The key fingers are the last three of the left hand. These determine whether the shot will be accurate or otherwise.
There is no hint of loosening the grip.

(VIII) GENE LITTLER (USA)

In the early stage of the downswing the left arm pulls the club down and being straight ensures that the right arm comes in to the side.
It is essential to become left hand conscious.

Bill Collins (USA)   *(Opposite) Gene Littler (USA)*

(IX) MAX FAULKNER (England)

The tucking-in of the right elbow ensures that the full force of the shot is generated and transmitted through the hands.
It is also a safeguard against the left hand being overpowered by the right.
At this point of the swing, the acceleration of clubhead speed is terrific.

(X) BOBBY LOCKE (South Africa)

No braking at impact. Club must be hit through.

Left hip moves out of the way to allow the hands to flow out after the ball without interruption.

Angle of shoulders indicates that the body has stayed behind the shot.

(XI) GEORGE WILL (Scotland)

Flowing action of arms and club have brought the body round in fluent fashion. Grip still firm, particularly the left hand.

The finish has the hall-mark of balance and poise—an accurate indicator of what went before.

(XII) SEBASTIAN MIGUEL (Spain)

Finger-prints of putting styles are as individualistic as the players holding the putters. There is no set method, but one feature is common to all brilliant putters. The grip is never tense. That is the quickest way to kill a sensitive touch.

The most popular grip is the reverse overlap.

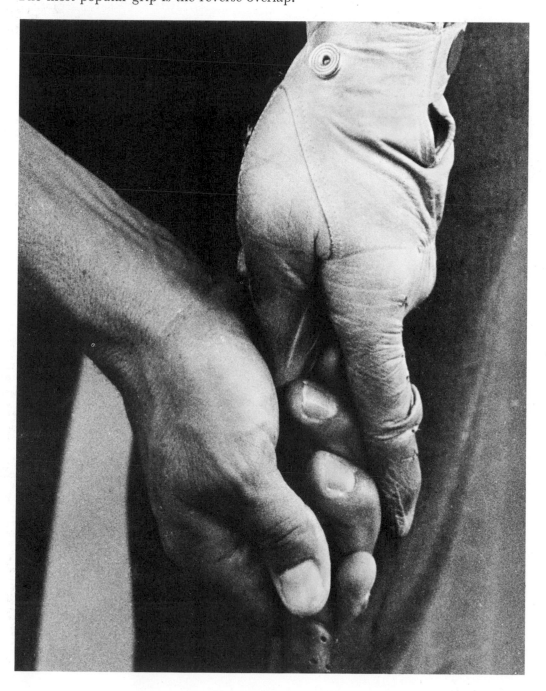

(XIII) PETER BUTLER (England)

In the backswing the putter is taken back low with slow rhythm and blade square to hole. No movement of head, shoulders or hips.

(XIV) GARY PLAYER (South Africa)

The putter strokes through the ball.

Blade hugs the ground.

Body action eliminated.

The mechanics of putting can be learnt, but in reality the only difference between good and bad putting is the mental attitude of the player. In short, putts are made "twixt the ears".

Index